Richard Reid

# GALLIPOLI 1915

Published by ABC Books for the
AUSTRALIAN BROADCASTING CORPORATION
GPO Box 9994 Sydney NSW 2001

Copyright © text Department of Veterans' Affairs 2002

*First published April 2002*
*Reprinted February 2003*

All rights reserved. No part of this publication
may be reproduced, stored in a retrieval system
or transmitted in any form or by any means,
electronic, mechanical, photocopying, recording
or otherwise, without the prior written permission
of the Australian Broadcasting Corporation.

National Library of Australia
Cataloguing-in-Publication entry
Reid, Richard
Gallipoli 1915.
ISBN 0 7333 1072 9.
1. World War, 1914-1918 - Campaigns - Turkey - Gallipoli
Peninsula - Pictorial works. 2. Public opinion - Australia.
I. Australian Broadcasting Corporation. II. Title.
940.426

*Designed by Melanie Feddersen, i2i design, Sydney*
*Set in Life 10.5/15pt*
*Colour reproduction by PageSet, Melbourne*
*Printed in Singapore by Tien Wah Press*

5 4 3 2

Bury the body — it has served its ends;
Mark the spot, but 'On Gallipoli'.
Let it be said 'he died'. Oh!
Hearts of Friends
If I am worth it, keep my memory.

*Every camp, hill and gully now has a distinctive Australian name … The position facing north is known as Walker's Ridge, and following the perimeter of defence right round until it strikes the coast to the south you are introduced in turn to Pope's Hill, Dead Man's Ridge, the Bloody Angle, Quinn's Post, Courtney's Post, McLaurin's Hill, Scott's Point, Johnstone's Jolly, Bolton's Hill and Point Rosenthal, each of these names recalling some incident of the campaign or some memory of peaceful times in 'Down Under'.*

[Ellis Ashmead-Bartlett, English war correspondent]

# CONTENTS

| | |
|---|---|
| INTRODUCTION | 1 |
| THE ALLIED NAVIES | 10 |
| THE LANDING | 22 |
| BATTLE | 38 |
| DAILY WARFARE | 48 |
| MEDICAL SERVICES | 60 |
| BEACHES AND HARBOURS | 70 |
| DAILY LIFE | 80 |
| DWELLINGS | 104 |
| EVACUATION | 114 |
| GALLIPOLI PORTRAITS | 120 |
| THE GALLIPOLI DRAWINGS OF CAPTAIN LESLIE HORE | 123 |
| REMEMBERING GALLIPOLI 1915-1930 | 134 |
| ACKNOWLEDGMENTS | 153 |
| BIBLIOGRAPHY | 154 |

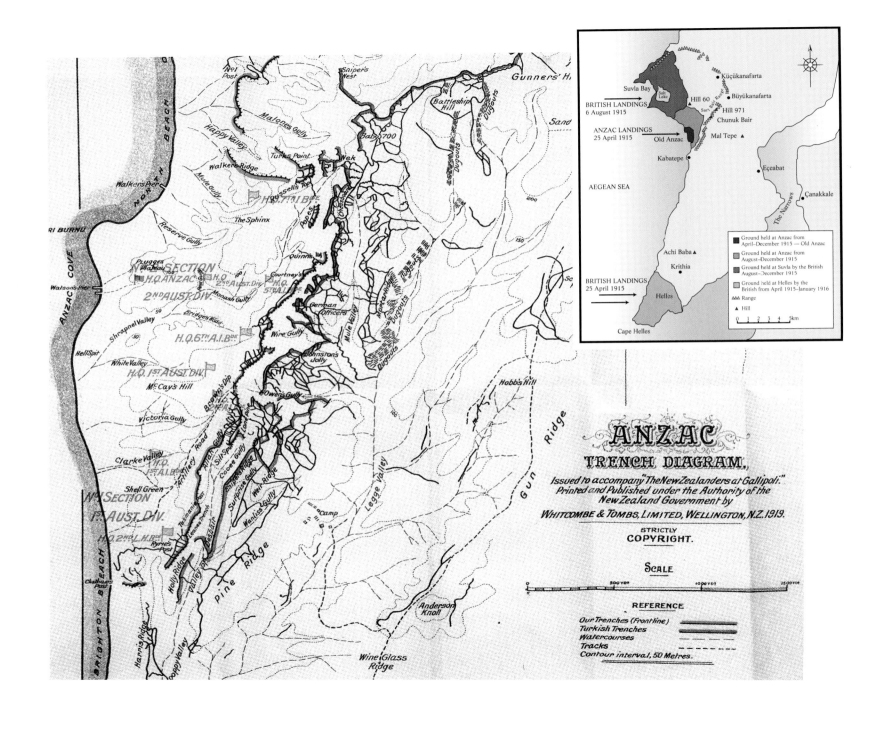

# INTRODUCTION

In 1948, Charles Bean, Australia's official historian of World War I, saw the future of the Gallipoli peninsula, Turkey, in these words:

*After perhaps all great wars — certainly after all modern ones — soldiers and relatives and, later, interested visitors have flowed to the battlefields; and one's mind could see Anzac, the most striking battlefield of that war, being the goal of pilgrimages from Britain and the Anzac countries, a calling place on Mediterranean tours, a regular stopping place for those who visited Egypt and the Holy Land and thence made their way by Damascus and the Taurus to Asia Minor, Constantinople and Greece.*

How right he was. For a few days each year around 25 April, the cemeteries and ravines of the old Australian positions at Gallipoli — the Anzac area — swarm with visitors. Most, although not all, are young backpackers from Australia and New Zealand who good-naturedly lie out in the open all night at the Anzac Commemorative Site at North Beach waiting for dawn and the Dawn Service. Once the memory of the famous landing has, again, been observed, the crowd moves off to Ari Burnu Cemetery, to walk along Anzac Cove beach and then makes its way up into the hills to Lone Pine. There, after choruses of 'We are Australian', accompanied by an Australian Defence Force band, all participate in a service of remembrance for the thousands of Australians whose graves and memorials are visible along the ridge line leading up from the Pine to the heights of Chunuk Bair. How do these Australians of the twenty-first century imagine the reality that was Gallipoli between April 1915 and January 1916, as they sing that old imperial refrain at the Dawn Service:

TOP: Surgeon Major Hinton, aged 103, a British India Army veteran, tells his war stories to five wounded Australian Gallipoli veterans, Glenelg, South Australia, 1916. (AWM H11602).

BOTTOM: *Fighting the Battle O'er Again*, from *The Sydney Mail*, 28 July 1915. The original caption spoke of how the deeds of the Australians at Gallipoli would 'long furnish subjects for thrilling stories'. (NLA).

*God of our fathers, known of old,*
*Lord of our far-flung battle-line,*
*Beneath whose awful Hand we hold*
*Dominion over palm and pine —*
*Lord God of Hosts, be with us yet,*
*Lest we forget — lest we forget!*

Charles Bean, Australian official war correspondent, and British journalist Ellis Ashmead-Bartlett (behind) on Imbros Island, near Gallipoli, 1915. (AWM A05382).

RIGHT: *Where the Australians Gained Imperishable Renown*, from The Sydney Mail, 16 June 1915. One of the first published photographs of Gallipoli 'taken by a Sydney quartermaster sergeant on the day of the historic landing'. (NLA).

Gallipoli was a 'striking battlefield', Bean wrote, and none knew that better than he. Week after week throughout 1915, as Australia's official war correspondent, he struggled to paint pictures in words for Australian readers hungry for any impression of the far away place where their husbands, fathers, sons, relatives and friends now lived and died:

*As you climb that ridge you can sit down anywhere for a rest, and you have out on your flank a wide sweeping beach, a perfect blue sea, and inland a stretch of beautiful country leading up to the hills ... I often go and sit there, or on a low hill further on, and rest my telescope on a bank in front, or on the low bough of a certain stumpy pine there, and gaze out into that country.*

By late May 1915 the Australian public were gaining another sense of 'that country', not from the journalist's skilful choice of adjectives but from the work of the sketcher and photographer. Drawings and photographs of life and battle at Gallipoli began appearing in the metropolitan weekly illustrated publications such as *The Sydney Mail*, *The Town and Country Journal*, *The Australasian* and *The Tasmanian Mail*. Of all these journals, *The Sydney Mail* offered the most extensive coverage of illustrations from the distant theatres of war.

From the outbreak of the war in August 1914 until the allied landings at Gallipoli on 25 April 1915, the *Mail* had, through the medium of photographs and drawings, taken its readers to the battlefields of France, Belgium, eastern Europe and the Middle East. The *Mail* also covered the recruitment of Australians for overseas military service in the new Australian Imperial Force (AIF) and then followed this force as it camped under the pyramids of Egypt in early 1915. Maps and pictures reported the British Royal Navy and French Navy's attempts in March 1915 to send a fleet through the straits of the Dardanelles to Constantinople, the capital of the Ottoman Empire. Finally, on 5 May 1915, *Mail* readers received their first visual impression of Gallipoli — a map of the Dardanelles region under the heading, 'Forcing the Dardanelles: Where Our Troops Landed'. A week later, the flat map had been turned by an unnamed *Mail* artist into a three-dimensional representation of Gallipoli and the adjacent Turkish mainland. Readers were now able to grasp something of the hilly nature of the western coast of the peninsula where the AIF had landed and to see its relationship with the straits of the Dardanelles, the objective of the whole attack.

Photographs from Gallipoli were slow in coming — the first did not appear in the *Mail* until 16 June. Until then, the paper turned to illustrators to capture the drama of the landing. These highly imaginative presentations were inspired by the first newspaper accounts about Australian soldiers, notably the dispatch of English war correspondent Ellis Ashmead-Bartlett, published in the Australian press on 8 May 1915. Bartlett's famous account was the first detailed description of Australian soldiers at the landing to reach Australia and, along with Charles Bean's first official dispatch, it had by 18 May been turned into a pamphlet and hurried into schools by the New South Wales Department of Public Instruction. A drawing entitled 'Bathing to the Accompaniment of Bursting Shells' appeared in the *Mail* on 19 May and showed Australians casually taking a swim at Gallipoli. Out to sea, warships of the Royal Navy stand guard off the coast while Turkish shells, ignored by the swimmers, explode in the water.

From the appearance of the first Gallipoli photograph in June until the end of 1915, the *Mail* published dozens of images of Gallipoli. Where did these photographs come from? Many, including the first, seem to have been sent back by soldiers who had taken cameras with them. Photos sent home to families were a source the *Mail* often acknowledged in captions. One of the first published photographs was titled 'Where the Australians Gained Imperishable Renown' and attributed to 'a Sydney quartermaster sergeant'. The caption claimed it was taken on 25 April and that it showed a hill recently taken from the Turks on which a wounded man was receiving attention from his comrades.

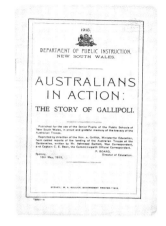

Within weeks of the landing, the Department of Public Instruction, New South Wales, published Ellis Ashmead-Bartlett's account, along with Charles Bean's first official dispatch. (SLNSW).

LEFT: *The Soldier's Kodak*, from *The Sydney Mail*, 19 May 1915. It was claimed that the camera could 'be loaded with Kodak film in broad daylight, much as you load a revolver'. (NLA).

RIGHT: *The Dardanelles Campaign: Scenes at Anzac,* from *The Sydney Mail,* 17 November 1915. The drawing was described as 'A glimpse of Mule Gully, with a hospital ship lying out at sea'. (NLA).

Another rich source of photographs for the Australian press came from the British official photographers on Gallipoli, notably those of the British Admiralty. The photos, although sometimes obviously posed, point to an aspect of the campaign nowadays often overlooked in Australia in both commemorative ceremonies and other presentations — the allied force on Gallipoli was a multinational one. Surrounding the Australians on the peninsula were soldiers from France, French colonial Africa, India, Nepal and Newfoundland, not to mention England, Ireland, Scotland, Wales and New Zealand, men of the Maori nation included. The official Admiralty photos were taken with an eye to press publication and with a requirement to reflect the different nationalities and arms of the services involved in the campaign.

One Gallipoli veteran who was well aware of this multinational element was Charles Bean. His dispatches naturally highlight the role the Australians were playing in the campaign but he also made frequent reference to other nationalities, including the Turks. One of Bean's most moving accounts described the burial of Major Charles Herbert Villiers-Stuart, 56th Punjabi Rifles, Indian Army. Villiers-Stuart, an Irishman serving with the British India Army, was attached to Anzac Headquarters as an intelligence officer:

*You could hear the voice of the clergyman:*

*Now the battle day is o'er,*
*Jesu in thy gracious keeping,*
*Leave we here thy warrior sleeping.*

*… strong men lift him tenderly from the stretcher. The congregation melts … and there we leave him to the waves and the sea-breezes amid the little wooden crosses on that shrapnel-swept point.*

In 1944, late in World War II, Bean wrote his now almost forgotten 'Anzac Requiem' for reading on Anzac Day. His first paragraphs roamed across all those places in both world wars where Australians lost their lives and are buried. Then he came to what he felt Australians should remember of 25 April 1915:

*We recall, too, those staunch friends who fought beside our men on the first Anzac Day — our brothers from New Zealand who helped to create the name of Anzac — the men of the Royal Navy, and of the 29th and other British divisions — the Indian mountain gunners — and our brave French Allies.*

Another typical *Sydney Mail* presentation of life on Gallipoli showed a much less known side of the soldiers' reaction to the campaign — personal drawings. On 17 November 1915, a page called 'Scenes at Anzac' showed three photographs titled 'A Soldier's Snapshots at Anzac'. This was very much what *Mail* readers had become used to seeing virtually every week — pictures sent from Gallipoli of the scrub covered gullies of the Anzac position with Australian soldiers' bivvies (bivouacs). Above these snapshots, however, was a drawing called 'A Glimpse of Mule Gully with a Hospital Ship Lying Out at Sea'. It was signed by 'LFSH'.

'LFSH' were the initials of Captain Leslie Fraser Standish Hore of the 8th Light Horse Regiment, AIF. Hore, an Englishman born in India and an Oxford graduate, served at Gallipoli with his unit from

A blinded Gallipoli veteran, Private Frank Downes, 9th Battalion, AIF (right), being helped off the ship at Sydney by Chaplain-Colonel George Rowe, August 1915. (AWM H11572).

RIGHT: On 24 August 1915, Chaplain-Colonel Rowe, assisted by Private Frank Downes, gave a talk on Gallipoli illustrated by slides at Town Hall, Sydney. (SLNSW).

mid-May 1915 until he was wounded on 7 August at the famous charge at the Nek. He returned to Anzac on 28 September and remained there until the evacuation on 19–20 December. During his time on Gallipoli, Hore undoubtedly wrote many letters home to his wife. More interestingly, he also sent back a series of drawings, some in watercolour, others in ink and pencil. It seems that these drawings, which cover many aspects of his time on Anzac, came home with his letters, as the fold marks are still visible.

Looking at Hore's drawings all these years later something surprising about Gallipoli emerges — those who served there experienced it in colour! Black and white photographs have formed much of our visual sense of the reality of Gallipoli. Brilliant and striking though some of these photographs can be, they can fail to convey the full impact of the original scene. For example, there is one photograph taken by Bean of Australians looking at the glory of a Gallipoli sunset. Where the sun should be, there is only a glowing white glaze. In his colour pencil drawing, 'Tea on the Terrace', Hore captures the mood of such sunsets in a way not available to even the most skilful photographer on the peninsula. In the foreground four soldiers are boiling the billy while the sun sinks red into the sea beside the mountainous nearby islands of Imbros and Samothrace. It is a moment of peace, described by many in words, but caught beautifully by this forgotten Gallipoli sketcher. It is perhaps no surprise that Hore's wife sent some of his efforts to *The Sydney Mail* where two of them were re-drawn for reproduction.

By late December 1915 the AIF had left Gallipoli and what had happened there was consigned to memory and commemoration. Even during the campaign personal memory had already begun to play its part in the telling in Australia of the story of Anzac. Throughout 1915 wounded soldiers arrived home with first-hand accounts of war and the *Mail's* artist imagined them holding forth to eager listeners. As early as August 1915 a public presentation by 'Chaplain-Colonel G E Rowe — just returned from Egypt' took place at Sydney Town Hall. It was billed as offering 'Electric Views' of various locations in Egypt and 'The Shores of Gallipoli'. Illustration and memory were brought together on this occasion by an address from Private Frank Downes, a returned soldier who had been blinded by a bullet while serving on Gallipoli with the 9th Battalion.

By 1916 the desire to mark the significance of Gallipoli gripped the country. April 25 was now 'Anzac Day' and official programs, such as that published by the South Australian government, featured imaginative illustrations of the landing. Such was the appeal of the name 'Anzac' that the Commonwealth government brought in legislation restricting its use for any but commemorative purposes. Dozens of small businesses and individuals, returned 'Anzacs' among them, began making applications to the Attorney General for permission to use the magnetic word 'Anzac' in their advertising. The real experience of Gallipoli was being transformed into the stuff of legend and myth making.

At the heart of the legend, however, lay the old battlefield. As soon as the war was over, a British Graves Registration Unit whose task was to seek out and identify the burial places of the British and Dominion dead, was despatched to Gallipoli. There, in February and March 1919, Charles Bean and the members of his 'Gallipoli Mission' visited them. Bean rode and tramped over all the old battle sites with his photographer, Hubert Wilkins, investigating the unsolved riddles of the campaign and musing over the future of this 'striking battlefield'. Characteristically, while he spent the bulk of his time dealing with Australian matters, he remained conscious of the catastrophe that Gallipoli had been for other nationalities. A telling photograph shows the view down the valley of the Aghyl Dere in the Anzac area where one of the great tragedies of Gallipoli occurred – the destruction of a brigade of British soldiers under Brigadier General A H Baldwin on the morning of 10 August 1915. It has been suggested that upwards of a thousand British soldiers were slain there in the great Turkish counter-attack that drove British Empire forces forever from the heights of Chunuk Bair. Bean's 1919 photograph shows some of their remains beneath a cleared area known as The Farm:

*We came across the remains of men, thick; all below the seaward edge of the shelf [of The Farm]. The slope for a hundred yards down was simply covered with them. Those on the right were mostly of the Royal Irish Rifles; then some Wilts and Hants [Wiltshire Regiment,*

*Hampshire Regiment]. As far as the northern edge of The Farm slope the bodies of Tommies were thick – their helmets everywhere ... For the first time in our mission to Gallipoli, the scenes we looked on that afternoon 'got us down' ... For some reason the dissolution of the human remains in that lofty area was not quite so complete as at Old Anzac; and the number that must have been trapped, and the hopelessness of the situation on those steep ridges when once they were caught there, does not bear thinking about.*

By 1926 the cemeteries and memorials of Gallipoli, constructed by the Imperial War Graves Commission (now Commonwealth War Graves Commission), were complete. Few families could afford the long journey from Australia to visit the grave of a vanished father, son or brother but some did. In the 1920s beside the grave of Private George Grimwade, Australian Army Medical Corps, at the Shrapnel Valley Cemetery a stone was 'placed here in ever-loving remembrance by his parents, April 1922'. It is the image of those cemeteries with their neat rows of grave markers recording names, units and ages that most remains with the modern visitor after an Anzac Day journey to Gallipoli.

An unidentified Australian officer, in France 1918, wears an 'A' on his shoulder flash, indicating that he served at Gallipoli. (AWM E03886).

Other images show that for the veterans themselves there were many other occasions to recall, probably with mixed emotions. For Tasmanian veterans one such day was 20 October 1914 when the first contingent of that state's recruits for the AIF sailed from Hobart. Some of those who had sailed out of the Derwent on that historic occasion were photographed with their children at their first reunion at the Hobart War Memorial on 18 October 1930. Above them they placed a flag with the symbol 'A' for Anzac and it is likely that most of them fought at Gallipoli. Each of them thereafter would have been entitled to wear on his unit colour patch a brass 'A' signifying service during the campaign either on the peninsula itself or on the lines of communication stretching through the nearby Greek islands of Imbros and Lemnos back to Egypt.

Where are all those images now and what is their importance as Australians seem, at the beginning of a new century, committed to continue their engagement with the idea of

Anzac and Anzac Day? The images are to be found in the great national and state archival collections. Pre-eminent among these is the Australian War Memorial with about 6,000 photographs taken by individual soldiers, war correspondents such as Charles Bean or by the British official photographers. Scanning through them, it is possible to pick out dozens that originally appeared in 1915 in *The Sydney Mail* and other illustrated publications. Other material, such as Major Hore's drawings and that relating to the use of the word 'Anzac', can be found in institutions such as the Mitchell Library, Sydney, or the National Archives of Australia, Canberra.

Waiting for news from Gallipoli outside the offices of *The Argus* newspaper, Melbourne, late 1915.
(AWM A03152).

The significance of these images is two-fold. Firstly, they are the most direct way now in which we can see for ourselves what Gallipoli looked like to those who were there as well as those who interpreted it second hand in Australia. Without those images we have only the written word, powerful though that can be, to convey the visual reality of such an important event for Australia. Secondly, some of these images reveal a Gallipoli that is now rarely acknowledged on Anzac Day — Bean's Gallipoli where Gurkhas, Indians, New Zealanders, Englishmen and others rubbed shoulders with their Australian comrades. The images presented in this book, along with the written words of some who served at or wrote about Gallipoli, will help bring the viewer closer to an experience to which we still return as a way of defining who we are.

*Here's health to the Navy*

# THE ALLIED
# NAVIES

What is often forgotten in Australia about the Gallipoli campaign is that it actually began as a naval operation. Originally the British conceived of the action as a naval offensive through the Straits of the Dardanelles to Constantinople (Istanbul) — the aim was to knock the Ottoman Empire (Turkey), Germany's ally, out of the war . A great fleet of battleships from the British Royal Navy and the French Navy, with attendant cruisers and destroyers, were to sail across the Sea of Marmora, anchor off Constantinople and fire a few broadsides to strike fear and panic into the heart of the Turkish government causing Turkey to surrender. The Turkish defences of the straits, however, did not crumble, despite the efforts of the allied naval guns and minesweepers. A number of attacks, culminating in the great combined sweep of the allied battle fleet up the straits on 18 March 1915, failed to dislodge the Turkish shore batteries or rid the waters of hostile mines. After a loss of three battleships, with three more badly damaged, the naval offensive was called off. Hundreds of sailors, mainly French, had been killed or drowned.

After 18 March the task of silencing the Turkish defences of the Dardanelles was handed over to the British and French armies. Troops were to be landed on the Gallipoli peninsula, the defences captured and the battleships would then be able to head through to Constantinople. From April 1915 to January 1916, as the British Empire and French armies struggled without success on the peninsula, the ships of the Royal Navy and the aircraft of the Royal Naval Air Service supported them in every way possible. To Australians like Major Oliver Hogue of the 6th Light Horse Regiment the men of the Royal Navy were simply 'miracle workers.'

British sailors cleaning the decks of a battleship in the eastern Mediterranean under Lord Nelson's famous order to his men at the Battle of Trafalgar, 21 October 1805. (AWM G00698).

On 13 December 1914, the British submarine *B11*, under the command of Lieutenant Norman Holbrook, penetrated the minefields of the Dardanelles and sank the Turkish battleship *Messudiyeh*. Holbrook was awarded the Victoria Cross.

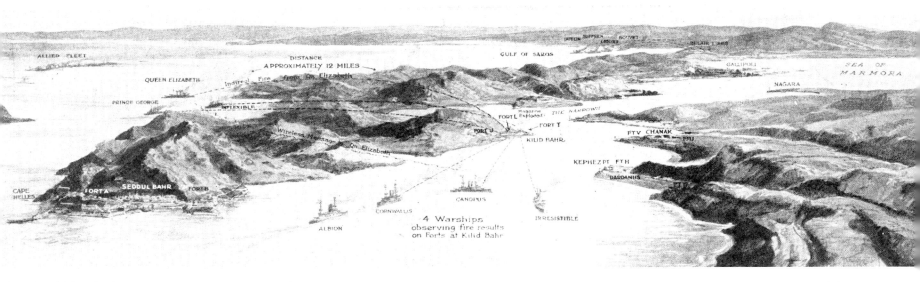

This contemporary *Diagrammatic View of the Entrance to the Dardanelles* showed what the British and French navies were doing in early 1915 to break through the Turkish defences at the straits.

LEFT: The British battleship HMS *Irresistible*, listing after it had struck a mine on 18 March 1915 during the great naval attack on the Turkish shore defences of the Dardanelles.

British soldiers in 1919 sitting on a large Turkish gun in one of the forts that had defended the entrance to the Dardanelles. (AWM H00230).

LEFT: The grave of Chief Petty Officer Charles Varcoe, Royal Australian Navy, of the Australian submarine *AE2*, Taurus Mountains, Turkey. The *AE2*, which got through the Dardanelles on 25 April 1915, was sunk by the Turks on 30 April. The crew members were taken prisoner; four were later to die in captivity. (AWM P1645.003).

*In those months of midsummer, it was a thrilling sight to see those great ships, often mirrored on the calm waters of the blue Aegean, rocking to the recoil of the mighty guns, as the shells went tearing overhead, and then burst on their targets, and then the vessels would be temporarily obscured by the billowing smoke from the discharge of their guns.*

[Captain Walter Belford, 11th Battalion, AIF]

*Meanwhile, here's health to the Navy, that took us there, and away:*
*Lord! They're miracle-workers — and fresh ones every day!*
*My word! Those Mids in the cutters! Aren't they properly keen!*
*Don't ever say old England's rotten — or not to us, who've seen!*

[From 'Anzac', Major Oliver Hogue, 6th Light Horse Regiment, AIF]

The battleship HMS *Cornwallis*, the last ship to leave Gallipoli in the evacuation of 19–20 December 1915, firing on Turkish positions. (AWM H10388).

RIGHT: British midshipmen off for an afternoon picnic on Imbros Island. Midshipmen such as these commanded the boats that took the Anzacs ashore on 25 April 1915. (AWM G00389).

LEFT: Church service in the Dardanelles aboard HMS *Queen Elizabeth*, under the muzzles of the warship's 15-inch guns. Ellis Ashmead-Bartlett wrote that its guns made 'every other gun you have ever seen look ridiculous and contemptible'.

THE ALLIED NAVIES

*The ships and shipping were of great interest to the troops, marooned as they were far from all the social amenities. Their comings and goings and their manoeuvres were practically the only novelties in the lives of the boys; the boats were the only links that bound them to the outside world.*

[Captain Walter Belford, 11th Battalion, AIF]

TOP: Anzac reinforcements on the deck of a North Sea fishing trawler preparing to go ashore in early May 1915. The trawlers were a familiar sight at Gallipoli. (AWM P1287.11.11).

LEFT: Survivors from the battleship HMS *Triumph* arrive alongside HMS *Lord Nelson*. On 25 May 1915, a German submarine torpedoed and sank the *Triumph* off the Anzac area.

RIGHT: On 27 May 1915, the battleship HMS *Majestic* was torpedoed and sunk off Helles. An Australian soldier wrote: 'It is stupefying, those massive ships stricken so suddenly. It is woe to us, for the help of their great guns feels almost like human support'. (NLA).

BOTTOM: The Captain's Clerk of HMS *Triumph* who swam about with the ship's ledger until a destroyer rescued him. (AWM G00200).

*What we saw was a little crowd of our small craft, with others, hastening up from all over the sea towards a centre — and that centre was a great object, whose shape it was at first glance a little difficult to recognise. It could not be an enemy's submarine — it was some different business than that — it could not be that it was one of our ships that was sinking — that the enemy's submarine or mine had found her? Somebody behind me was saying something about, 'Ten minutes ago — torpedo — on the starboard side'. 'What ship?', we asked — 'No! Don't say it was the* Triumph? *Not the old friend who has stood by us all these weeks — on which we have never called in vain? Not the* Triumph *— that poor wounded thing out there — dying whilst we looked at her.*

[Charles Bean, official dispatch]

Remarkable Picture of H.M.S. Majestic Sinking.

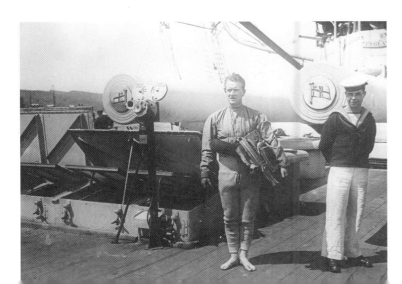

THE ALLIED NAVIES

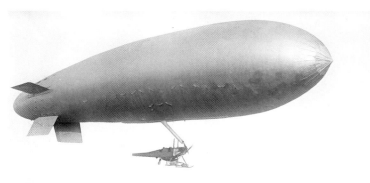

*Samson liked to go up in the first light of the morning, and having waved to the British soldiers in the trenches he flew on up the peninsula to catch the Turks around their cooking fires. Then he would return in the last light of the evening to shoot up the enemy camel drivers and bullock carts as they set out for the front.*

[Alan Moorehead, Gallipoli historian]

TOP LEFT: Commander Charles Samson, Royal Naval Air Service, standing beside his single seat Nieuport 10, before flying on a reconnaissance over the Turkish lines. (AWM G00523).

TOP RIGHT: The liners *Olympic* and *Aquitania*, fitted out for use as a hospital ship and troop transport, arriving at Mudros harbour, Lemnos Island. (AWM G00608).

LEFT: A British naval airship returning to its base after a long flight over Gallipoli. (AWM H10339).

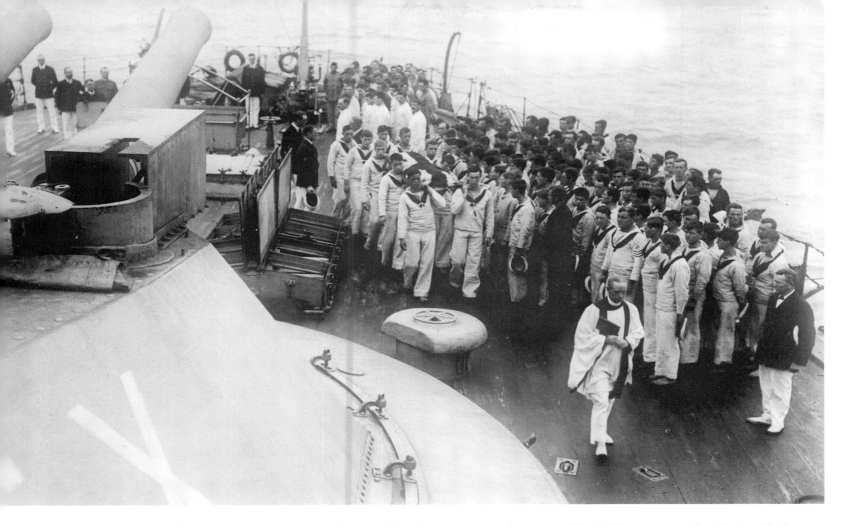

*As a spectacle ... it is superb. As I look out on the Bay of Mudros ... I see such an assembly of different types of warships, transports, and craft as has never been brought together before. The whole of this immense bay is studded with ships and small boats plying between them. They vary in size and shape from the mighty [HMS]* Queen Elizabeth, *with her eight 15-inch guns dominating the whole picture, to the little blue-painted fishing smacks of the islanders. Their number is too great to count even with the most powerful glasses. It would seem as if every type of warship and every type of transport which can possibly be spared from the other theatres of war have been collected here in Mudros Bay.*

[Ellis Ashmead-Bartlett, English war correspondent]

The burial of a British sailor at sea off Gallipoli. (AWM G00504).

*stick to it lads*

# THE LANDING

For years, Australian memory of the invasion of Gallipoli has fixed its gaze upon the beaches of the old Anzac position, particularly upon Anzac Cove. In reality, few men were killed as they landed: the real battle that developed was the battle to establish a defensible position and to hold off brave and determined Turkish counter-attacks that occurred inland along the ridges and tops of the steep gullies of that part of the Gallipoli peninsula. This was accomplished between 25 April and 3 May, a period called by Charles Bean, Australia's official historian, the 'Landing'. Bean estimated the total Australian and New Zealand casualties, along with those of the men of the Royal Naval Division who supported the Anzacs, for those eight days at 8,500. Of these, an estimated 2,300 were killed or died of wounds. The Turks later estimated their casualties at 14,000.

Typical of the scale of the losses was the experience of the 16th Battalion from Western Australia. The main body of the 16th went ashore at Anzac Cove at 5.30 pm on 26 April and went straight up from the beach to positions in the hinterland at the head of Monash Valley. With one short rest, they fought there until May 3. On that day, those who answered their names at roll call numbered 307 officers and men out of 995 who had landed at Gallipoli.

Shortly after the initial Australian landings, soldiers of the British 29th Division started to come ashore on five beaches on the southern tip of the peninsula at what later became known as the Helles position. Something of the stubbornness of the opposition from the Turks can be gauged from the fact that 12 Victoria Crosses were awarded to British soldiers and sailors for their bravery on 25 April 1915. From 25–30 April, over 4,300 British soldiers became casualties. Of these over 1,000 were killed or died of wounds.

*Panoramic View of the Dardanelles*, from *The Sydney Mail*, 12 May 1915. Readers were informed 'that the point where the Australian troops landed, covering themselves in glory in doing so, is named Gaba Tepe'. (NLA).

LEFT: Australians practising landings at Lemnos Island, early April 1915. (AWM C02257).

*An Australian officer in one of the boats started to issue some orders, whereupon he was interrupted by [Midshipman] Longley-Cook who, in a clear authoritative voice with a polished English accent (so I was told by an Australian who was there) said to the officer, 'I beg your pardon, sir, but I am in charge of this tow'. The officer subsided into silence immediately and the troops in his boat were heard to mutter, 'Good on yer, kid!'*

[Midshipman Eric Bush, Royal Navy]

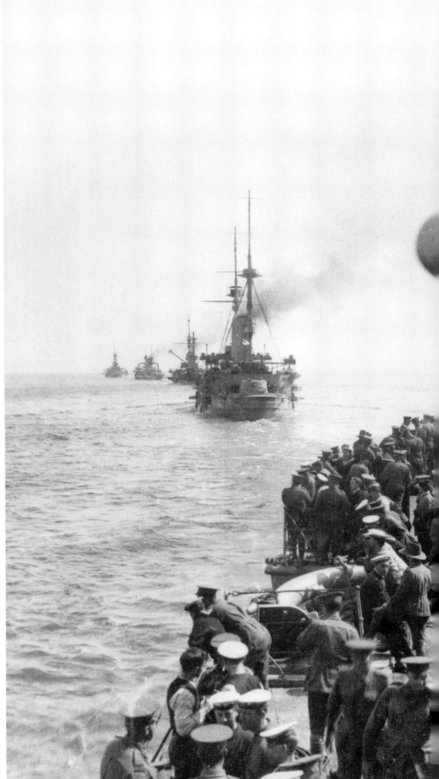

LEFT: Men of 11th Battalion, AIF, on the deck of the battleship HMS *London*, on their way to Gallipoli, 24 April 1915. Ahead are HM Ships *Queen* (leading), *Triumph*, *Prince of Wales* and *Bacchante*. (AWM A02465).

FAR LEFT: Australian troops in landing boats, being towed by a steam pinnace towards Gallipoli on the morning of 25 April 1915. (AWM P02194.005).

TOP: The 14th Battalion, AIF, transferring from a destroyer into landing boats in preparation for going ashore, 25 April 1915. (AWM A01214A).

BOTTOM: This photograph, originally captioned 'Anzac Beach at 6 a.m. April 25th 1915', may be one of the first photographs taken on Anzac. (AWM A03223).

RIGHT: Lance-Corporal Val Marshall, 4th Battalion, AIF, made this sketch of the landing of 25 April 1915. Marshall's sketch was described as showing countryside 'not unlike parts of the [Sydney] coastline near Curl Curl and north of Narrabeen'. (NLA).

*For conspicuous gallantry on the 25th April 1915, during the landing ... He had reached shelter when he saw a wounded man struggling in the surf, which was under heavy fire. Without hesitation, he turned back, reached the man in the water, and brought him successfully to shore, and subsequently to a place of shelter.*

[From official citation for the Distinguished Conduct Medal awarded to Private Cyril Green, 10th Battalion, AIF]

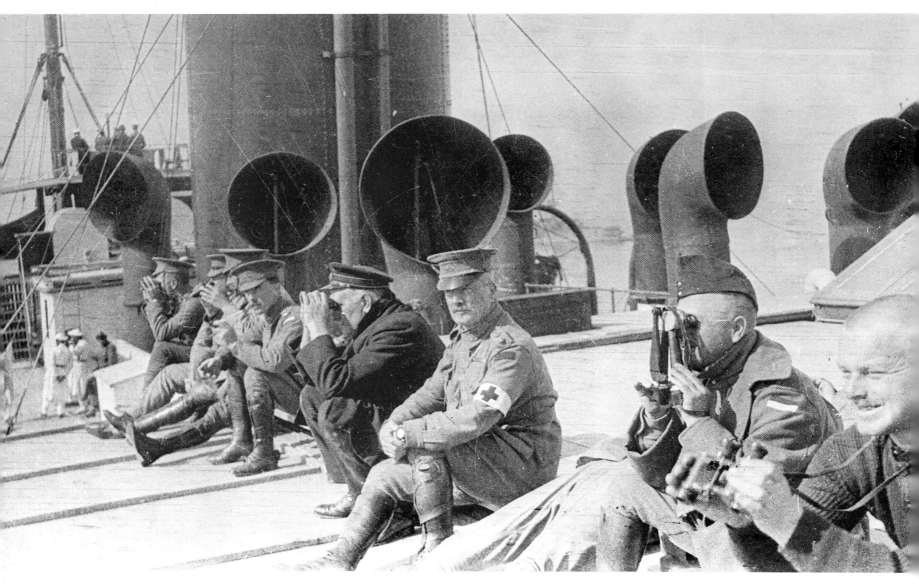

On the morning of 25 April 1915, officers of 2nd Field Ambulance, AIF, watch the landing at Anzac from the deck of the troopship *Mashoubra*. (AWM C01677).

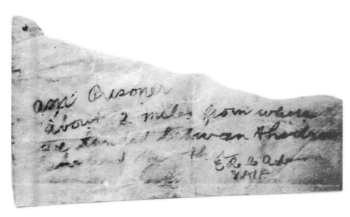

Private Edgar Robert Adams, 8th Battalion, AIF, who went missing on 25 April 1915. On 1 November 1915, a bottle washed up in Egypt with a message written by Adams, stating that he had been taken prisoner close to where his battalion had landed. No further record of his fate was ever traced. (AWM H14064 and H02397).

The 3rd Battalion, AIF, coming ashore at Gallipoli, 25 April 1915. The battalion, part of the 1st Brigade, landed between 5.30 and 7.30 a.m. The fighting by this stage was up in the hills behind the beach. (AWM A03224).

Sedd-el-Bahr fort and beach photographed from the *River Clyde* soon after it was run aground. Dead and wounded can been seen in the barge and the dark mass on the beach in the centre are soldiers pinned down by Turkish machine gun fire from the fort. (AWM A03076).

RIGHT: *The Historic Landing from the* River Clyde *at Seddul Bahr, Gallipoli, April 25th* 1915, from H W Wilson and J A Hammerton (eds), *The Great War*. This imaginative reconstruction of the British landing at V Beach, Helles, shows the men of the Munster Fusiliers and the Hampshire Regiment rushing out of the specially cut doors in the side of the steamer *River Clyde*. The ship was beached at 6.20 a.m. near the Turkish fort of Sedd-el-Bahr and the plan was to rush from the ship and pass along barges lashed together to form a pathway to the shore. In reality, as the accompanying photograph taken from the *River Clyde* shows, the barges did not reach the beach and dozens of men were killed as they tried to make their way across the barges and into the water. Those who reached the beach joined others, who had come ashore in small boats, under a sandbank where they sheltered from the intense Turkish machine gun fire coming from the fort. Commander Charles Samson, Royal Naval Air Service, flying above this scene later reported that the sea for 50 metres from the beach was 'absolutely red with blood'.

*Storming the Heights of Gaba Tepe,* from *The Sydney Mail*, 2 June 1915. The caption claimed that Colonel Doughty-Wylie led the Australians in this charge at the landing. This was completely wrong. On 26 April 1915, Lieutenant Colonel Charles Doughty-Wylie, Royal Welch Fusiliers, led a charge of British troops at Helles to clear the village of Sedd-el-Bahr. He died in this action and for his bravery was awarded a posthumous Victoria Cross. (NLA).

*In the early hours of the morning [26 April 1915] I heard the Officers going along amongst the men, saying 'Stick to it lads, don't go to sleep', and the cheerful reply would be 'No Sir, we won't go to sleep', and my heart swelled with admiration. I knew what the ordeal of the strenuous day before had been, and knew what pluck and determination was necessary to keep awake and alert through the long weary hours of the night, therefore I thought I was justified in being proud of being Australian ... give me Australians as comrades and I will go anywhere duty calls, and I hope to be pardoned for saying so, being one myself.*

[Private Roy Denning, 1st Field Company Engineers, AIF]

A 3rd Battalion, AIF, outpost during the battle of the 'Landing', 25 April to 3 May 1915. The photograph shows the scrub-covered country of the valleys and plateaus behind the landing beaches. These men have begun to dig in. (AWM A03227).

The first wounded Turkish prisoner taken at Anzac on the transport ship HMT *Galeka*, April 1915. (AWM P01287.005).

BOTTOM: Anzac Cove on the evening of 25 April 1915. The beach is now covered with men wounded in the battle in the hills inland, awaiting evacuation to the hospital ships. (AWM PS1659).

*Bloody Angle*, a drawing by Signaller Ellis Silas, 16th Battalion, AIF, showing his battalion in battle at the Bloody Angle, Gallipoli, dawn, 3 May 1915. Silas described how they sang 'Tipperary' as they charged up the hill and that the 'cries of the wounded, the tremendous fusillade of rifles and screaming of shells was indescribable'. (NLA).

The noise now is Hell ... Now some of the chaps are getting it — groans and screams everywhere, calls for ammunition and stretcher bearers, though how the latter are going to carry stretchers along such precipitous and sandy slopes beats me. Now commencing to take some of the dead out of the trenches; this is horrible; I wonder how long I can stand it.

[Signaller Ellis Silas, 16th Battalion, AIF]

*The Roll Call*, Ellis Silas. Silas depicts a company of the 16th Battalion at roll call on the morning of 9 May 1915. Between 25 April and 13 May 1915, the battalion suffered 757 casualties (dead, wounded and missing) out of 1,207 who had landed on the peninsula. (NLA).

The Roll is called — how heart-breaking it is — name after name is called; the reply, a deep silence which can be felt, despite the noise of the incessant cracking of rifles and screaming of shrapnel — there are few of us left to answer our names — just a thin line of weary, ashen-faced men, behind a mass of silent forms, once our comrades — there they have been for days, we have not had time to bury them.

[Signaller Ellis Silas, 16th Battalion, AIF, Gallipoli, 11 May 1915]

Dead soldiers covered by flags, being transferred from the hospital ship *Gascon* to a trawler for burial at sea. The *Gascon* was a well-known hospital ship at Gallipoli. (AWM A01859).

*Our Regiment has been cut to pieces*

# BATTLE

After the battle of the 'Landing' there were a number of major offensives on Gallipoli as the allied armies, British and French, sought to break through the Turkish lines and force their way to the Dardanelles. These were given titles such as Krithia and the 'August Offensive' which encompassed battles during August at Lone Pine, Chunuk Bair and Hill 60. The Turks also mounted heavy attacks with the object of driving the invaders into the sea but so great were their losses on these occasions that they stood mainly on the defensive.

Australian popular consciousness of battle at Gallipoli is dominated by the seeming futility and waste of life of many of the set-piece actions — especially by the charge of the dismounted Lighthorsemen of the 8th and 10th Light Horse Regiments at the Nek on 7 August 1915. It was around the events of that tragic episode that Peter Weir based the story of his film *Gallipoli*. Many other actions, however, deserve to be remembered. Among them is the charge of the four Victorian battalions — approximately 2,900 men — of the 2nd Brigade, AIF, in support of the British and French at Krithia, Helles, on 8 May 1915. A third of them were killed or wounded.

There are virtually no images of men engaging the enemy in the heat of battle. Artists for the Australian illustrated papers tried to make up for this deficiency, generally with highly imaginative drawings based on glowing newspaper accounts of Australian bravery triumphant over a less than formidable Turkish foe. Photographs, on the contrary, reflect the tragedy of loss through images such as piles of equipment once worn by the living or the bodies of the dead themselves.

*I write on board the hospital ship with a bullet through the bone of my right foot and another through my right shoulder, the latter only an inconvenience and the former a clean hole which ought to heal in about six weeks. Truly we have been through the valley of the shadow of death as our Regiment has been cut to pieces and all our officers killed or wounded except two, out of eighteen officers present twelve were killed and four wounded.*

[Captain Leslie Hore, 8th Light Horse Regiment, AIF]

The surviving members of 'D' Company, 7th Battalion, AIF, after the Battle of Krithia, 11 May 1915. 'D' Company would have landed on 25 April about 225 men strong. At the battles of the Landing and Krithia the 7th Battalion lost 795 men killed or wounded out of a total of 1,110 who served in the unit between 25 April and 18 May. (AWM A03308).

LEFT: Australian dead at the Battle of Krithia, Helles, 8 May 1915. Notice the flat nature of this battlefield by comparison with the Anzac area. (AWM C01079).

*Such was the attack of the 2nd Brigade at Krithia. In its actual attack, lasting over an hour, it had moved 1,000 yards across open moorland under heavy fusillade, the second half of the advance … being made in the teeth of rifle and machine gun fire such as Australians seldom again encountered during the war. Although in that short space they had lost 1,000 men, the advancing lines had shown not the least signs of wavering.*

[Charles Bean, official Australian war historian]

*When we had gone 2 miles in, word came back — enemy in strong numbers on our right. Word passed back to move around and attack. We slowly crept up the hill and they opened a fury of fire on us ... We rushed up the hill and I bayoneted one Turk, an old chap of 45 years. He had no papers on him ... Then we went down the other side and stormed a second hill. An explosive shell blew off the foresight of my rifle. Then with a party of volunteers I went with the Maoris to storm another hill. Somehow I got scattered from the rest and while passing a bush a gigantic Turk pounced on me and proceeded to crush me to death. However, before he got any further, Tipper, a mate of mine, bayoneted him. Almost immediately afterwards another Turk shot Tipper dead. He was revenged, however, as I manoeuvred around and shot his assailant dead.*

[Sergeant Harry Jackson 13th Battalion, AIF]

LEFT: *How Lance-Corporal Jacka Won Immortal Fame,* from *The Sydney Mail,* 4 August 1915. On 19–20 May, Albert Jacka, 14th Battalion, AIF, became the first Australian to be awarded a Victoria Cross in World War I. This illustration is a fairly imaginative portrayal of the nature of that action at Quinn's Post, Anzac. (NLA).

THE ARMISTICE: TURKS BURYING THEIR DEAD ON THE SLOPES OF SARI BAIR.

*The dead [Turks] fill the myrtle-grown gullies. One saw the result of machine-gun fire very clearly; entire companies annihilated — not wounded, but killed, their heads doubled under them with the impetus of their rush and both hands clasping their bayonets. It was as if god had breathed in their faces ...*

[Major Aubrey Herbert, British Intelligence Officer, Anzac Corps]

The bodies of 36 men of the 11th Battalion, AIF, killed during the fighting at Leane's Trench, 31 July to 1 August 1915. This Australian attack was part of the preparation for the major attack at Lone Pine that began on 6 August 1915. (AWM P02023.002).

LEFT: *The Armistice: Turks Burying Their Dead on the Slopes of Sari Bair*, from *The Sydney Mail*, 6 October 1915. On 24 May 1915 an armistice was held to bury the dead of the Turkish counter-attack of 19 May 1915. In that attack 3,000 Turks were killed and 7,000 wounded. (NLA).

*The men fell under furious fire. It was terrible; the men were falling like rabbits. Many were calling for mothers and sisters. They fell a good way, in many cases, from the Turkish lines. Sgt McKinley ... did very good work on the Peninsula. It was commonly believed that he was killed on that morning during the advance. He was never seen again.*

[Account from Australian Red Cross file concerning Sergeant Joseph McKinley, 15th Battalion, AIF]

*Of the 760 of the Wellington Battalion [New Zealand Expeditionary Force] who had captured the height that morning, there came out only 70 unwounded or slightly wounded men. Throughout that day not one had dreamed of leaving his post. Their uniforms were torn, their knees broken. They had had no water since the morning; they could talk only in whispers; their eyes were sunken; their knees trembled; some broke down and cried.*

[Charles Bean, official Australian war historian]

*[the dead] were lying everywhere, on top of the parapet ... in dugouts and communication trenches and saps, and it was impossible to avoid treading on them.*

[Private William Bendrey, 2nd Battalion, AIF]

The southern trench, Lone Pine, 8 August 1915. Bean described Lone Pine as 'sheer hand-to-hand fighting, certainly the heaviest of its kind in which Australian troops ever took part'. (AWM A04029).

LEFT: Looking back from Lone Pine to the jumping-off trench from which the 1st Australian Infantry Brigade began its attack on Turkish positions on 6 August 1915. During the Battle of Lone Pine, 6–9 August 1915, over 2,000 Australians and an estimated 6,930 Turks were killed or wounded. (AWM C01685).

FAR LEFT: A pile of personal equipment in Brown's Dip, 10 August 1915. Brown's Dip lay behind Lone Pine plateau and this equipment was taken from the dead and wounded after the Battle of Lone Pine. (AWM C01943).

*We gained about 400 yards in four days fighting, 1000 men killed and wounded. Land is very dear here.*

[Corporal James Watson, Auckland Mounted Rifles, New Zealand Expeditionary Force]

RIGHT: *Hand-to-hand Combat on the Heights of Sari Bair*, from *The Sydney Mail*, 15 September 1915. The 'August Offensive' of 6–10 August 1915 ended in a failure to break through to the Dardanelles. *The Sydney Mail's* illustration of this desperate struggle suggests that the Anzacs somehow gained battle superiority over the kind of cringing enemy soldiers shown here. (NLA).

BATTLE

45

*Dashing Maoris in a Thrilling Night Action*, from *The Sydney Mail*, 10 Nov 1915. This action occurred in the dark of 6 August 1915 as one of the opening attacks of the 'August Offensive'. The Maori Contingent historian wrote: 'This was their chance for fame. They went grimly for those Turks … they burst into a tremendous *haka* when they had cleared the trenches — "Ka mate, ka mate, ka ora, ka ora" — then silence'. (NLA).

*The battle cries … were for the Turks the sonorous, deep-voiced 'Allah, Allah' or 'Voor' ('God, God', 'Strike'); while the New Zealanders often used to shout: 'Eggs is cooked'. This apparently irrelevant, unwarlike slogan had its origin in Egypt. There, on field days in the desert, when the men halted to rest, Egyptians would appear magically with primitive kitchens and the cry of 'Eggs is cooked'.*

[Aubrey Herbert, British Intelligence Officer, Anzac Corps]

*For the order has come that we are to move to the forefront of battle, to enter the scorching flames of the firing line. For many days have we been quite ready. We Maoris are now off to strike — to finish what we came here for. The head officers of our party are here after greeting us, and are now instructing us in methods of warfare. Your letter of love has come to me. I am well; my only grief is I hear nothing but the English voice. It is so; therefore, I must not grieve. I now feel my spirit, my soul, my whole body are not mine. Never mind.*

[Private Huirua Rewha, Maori Contingent, New Zealand Expeditionary Force]

The last great battles of the Gallipoli campaign were fought in the Suvla area. In the late afternoon of 21 August 1915, the men of the British 2nd Mounted Division — 'Peyton's Yeomanry' — in failing light and with enemy shells bursting over them, advanced across the Salt Lake at Suvla. The British attack failed and over 5,000 were killed or wounded.

*That day I saw an unforgettable sight. The dismounted Yeomanry attacked the Turks across the salt lakes of Suvla Bay. Shrapnel burst over them continuously; above their heads there was a sea of smoke. Away to the north by Chocolate Hill fires broke out on the plain. The Yeomanry never faltered. On they came through the haze of smoke in two formations, column and extended. Sometimes they broke into a run, but they always came on. It is difficult to describe the feelings of pride and sorrow with which we watched this advance, in which so many of our friends and relations were playing their part.*

[Aubrey Herbert, British Intelligence Officer, Anzac Corps]

*An ordinary day of shelling,
bombing and sniping*

# DAILY WARFARE

In his regular dispatches from Gallipoli, Charles Bean often referred to the constant danger facing those who served there, no matter where they found themselves in the Anzac position. Many paths leading to the front line trenches on the ridges were in sight of Turkish snipers. Turkish shells fell daily on positions from the beaches up through the back rest areas in the valleys. Bombing duels were frequent and Bean wrote of one day during which two 'Maorilanders' threw 570 bombs at an opposing Turkish trench at Quinn's Post — 'and kept twenty yards of head-cover … burning for a whole night and day'.

Even during relatively quiet periods death and wounding were commonplace. The 22nd Battalion, AIF, arrived on Anzac in early September 1915. Bean described the period from their arrival until the final evacuation of Anzac on the night of 19–20 December 1915, as one during which there occurred at Anzac 'no heavy fighting'. Nonetheless, the 22nd suffered 43 dead and 285 wounded. In a similarly quiet 24 days in the front line trenches, the 28th Battalion had 22 dead and 46 wounded.

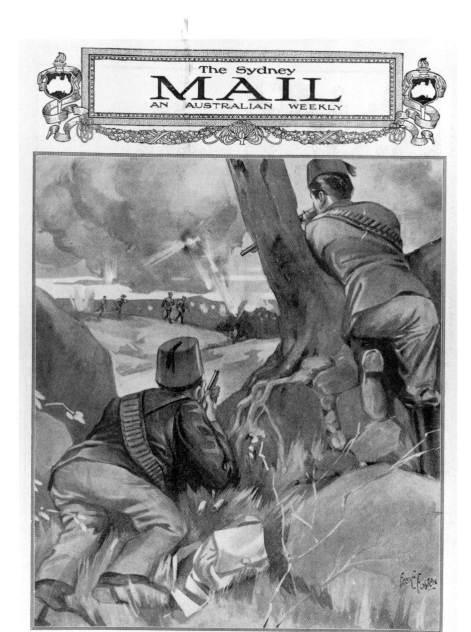

*Today, a dry, sleepy day, is quiet as any we have had; standing outside my quarters I have counted thirteen rifle shots within the last minute; of course many could not be heard. Thirty-seven shots were heard one minute, and seventy-six the next: they were practically all Turkish. This is what goes on day and night, without ceasing, in the intervals between the real fights. ...*

[Charles Bean, official dispatch]

*The Snipers*, from *The Sydney Mail* 21 July 1915. The Australians here are depicted as walking bravely and unconcernedly on the open battlefield while hidden Turkish snipers prepare to pick them off. (NLA).

RIGHT: An Australian sniper position. (AWM A03301).

*The post on the high side of the valley nearest the Turks was called Sniper's Post, and from there lots of us used to do quite a bit of shooting. The post was fitted up with five or six loop-holes through which we shot. As time went on 'Jacko' [the Turks] found this post and would fire at us quite as much as we fired at him. Unfortunately for us he had telescopic sights — which we didn't have, and with his glasses found the hole through which we observed. With great accuracy he fixed a rifle and trained it on this spot. One morning when I was in this particular post, a young chap named Cambden, named each of these loop-holes in turn, 'England', 'Egypt', 'Lemnos Beach', 'Australia', meaning that if we opened the loop-hole so named we would get wounded slightly or severely, according to the plate we moved. He chose 'England', opened the loop-hole and looked through. Sure enough a bullet came through and struck his eyebrow, breaking the bone. He went to hospital in England. Though he was badly wounded, we thought him lucky in leaving Gallipoli, as conditions there were terrible.*

[Sergeant Hector Haslam, 11th Battalion, AIF]

Australian loophole plate used for protection, showing enemy bullet marks made within a few days of its installation, July 1915. (AWM A01002).

LEFT: An Australian soldier operating a periscope rifle with a cut-out of the German Emperor, Kaiser Wilhelm II, mounted above trench level to supply a target for the Turkish snipers. (AWM H03488).

RIGHT: A captured Turkish sniper showing the camouflage he used to conceal himself. (AWM G00377A).

*Tuesday, September 28th, Nothing unusual to report today; just an ordinary day of shelling, bombing and sniping.*

[Seaman Joseph Murray, Hood Battalion, Royal Naval Division]

Australians practising bomb throwing. Bean wrote 'The good cricketer is the man for the bomb'. (AWM G00406).

BOTTOM: An Indian Mountain Battery in action at the back of Quinn's Post, Gallipoli. The Indian batteries were the first ashore to support the Anzacs on 25 April 1915. (AWM A03150).

RIGHT: A French siege gun at Helles firing towards the Asiatic coast of Turkey in an attempt to silence an enemy gun called 'Weary Willie'. (AWM G00581).

*Karm Singh [Indian Mountain Battery] would hear the order shouted from above, and would pass it on down below ... Karm Singh was passing down his orders when an orderly from his battery walked down the trench. The orderly noticed that Karm Singh was sitting close up against the side of the trench, with his head near the wall and his hand over his eyes, as if he had a headache. 'What is the matter, Karm Singh?' he asked, 'Oh, it's nothing; don't worry. I am quite able to pass messages', was the answer and the orderly passed along on his business ... Some time later when the business in hand was finished, they went down and had a look at Karm Singh. They found he had been shot through both eyes ... Karm Singh could still speak, if he could not see — that was all he cared for until his job was finished.*

[Charles Bean, official dispatch]

We were the centre of a high explosive bombardment ... how one loathes the sound of a high explosive humming towards one; if it lands near you, you are done; you cannot evade it like you can shrapnel; it tears through everything, and the wounds from it are too horrible for words.

[Lieutenant Colonel Cyril Allanson, 1/6th Gurkha Rifles, British India Army]

General Sir Ian Hamilton, Commander-in Chief, Mediterranean Expeditionary Force, decorating three French officers with the British Military Cross for 'bravery in the field'. (AWM G00490).

BOTTOM: A French soldier going out to help a wounded comrade, Helles. (AWM G00472).

French soldiers sorting out the kits of dead and wounded comrades.

BOTTOM: The 22nd Battalion, AIF, in early September 1915, soon after its arrival on Gallipoli, moving up to the firing line at Lone Pine. (AWM C02443).

*These troops came to the tired, and somewhat haggard garrison of Anzac, like a fresh breeze from the Australian bush. 'Great big cheery fellows, whom it did your heart good to see', wrote an Australian. 'Quite the biggest lot I have ever seen'.*

[Charles Bean, official Australian war historian]

*Out across the sea the exquisite last lights of sunset were just fading over Imbros. The old volcanic cone was showing out dark-grey against them. As we stood there amongst the frail wooden crosses we could hear the 'clink! clink!' of the mules along a path above … you could see their dark shapes passing with the Indians leading them … Some man passed along the path below us whistling. Suddenly the whistling stopped when he heard the voice of the clergyman, and knew what this dark crowd meant … You could hear the voice of the clergyman:*

> *Now the battle day is o'er,*
> *Jesu in thy gracious keeping,*
> *Leave we here thy warrior sleeping.*

*… strong men lift him tenderly from the stretcher. The congregation melts … and there we leave him to the waves and the sea-breezes amid the little wooden crosses on that shrapnel-swept point …*

[Charles Bean, official dispatch]

Australians and British Indian Army troops (Sikhs) watching Turkish prisoners in a prisoner of war cage in the Anzac area. (AWM C02712).

RIGHT: *How We Are Fighting the Turks*, from *The Sydney Mail*, 22 December 1915. When the Australians first landed on Gallipoli they had little respect for the Turks. However, during the campaign this attitude changed and the caption to this photograph reads, in part 'This [photograph] ... strikingly illustrates the attitude of the Australians towards the Turks in Gallipoli. Each recognising in the other a fair fighter and a brave enemy'. (NLA).

LEFT: Padre William McKenzie, Salvation Army, 4th Battalion, burying a soldier in Shrapnel Gully, Anzac, 24 May 1915. (AWM H15688).

*Murphy's at heaven's gate*

# MEDICAL
# SERVICES

Families back in Australia were naturally concerned about the treatment of the wounded and the Australian illustrated papers were quick to pick up on the work of the medical services at Gallipoli. Photographs of stretcher bearers on the nearby islands of Lemnos were among the first to be published and the story of Private John Simpson Kirkpatrick, 3rd Field Ambulance, AIF — the 'Man with the Donkey' — has become one of the most enduring of Australians at war.

The plight of the wounded during major actions was one of the most tragic stories of the campaign. Given the hilly and rugged nature of the terrain, and the presence of thousands of soldiers trying to battle their way upwards to the front line, stretcher bearers often found their work greatly impeded. Many badly wounded men had to lie out for hours before being carried down to dressing stations. Even there, the sheer crush of numbers led to evacuation bottlenecks to the hospital ships offshore.

At Lemnos Island, 100 kilometres from Gallipoli and one of the major allied bases, large Australian, British and Canadian tent hospitals were established for the sick and wounded — although many men were shipped to Egypt, Malta and even England. Later in the campaign, Sarpi Camp at Lemnos was also used as a place where the exhausted and rundown battalions from the peninsula could rest and recover.

A feature of the medical services off the peninsula, was the presence of women — the nurses of the Australian Army Nursing Service and their British and Canadian counterparts. The nurses of the hospital ships and the shore-based hospitals were the first Australian women in World War I to be exposed to the broken bodies of men subjected to the effects of bullets, bombs and jagged pieces of exploded shell.

Australian stretcher-bearers carrying a wounded man from the Chailak Dere, one of the valleys of the Sari Bair range, down to the beach, September 1915. (AWM C024220).

At last we got to the gully, down which I made my way with scores of the wounded to the beach. Most of the way down we were being fired at by snipers but barring a graze on my hip I escaped scot-free, others, however, not being so lucky for I saw two stretcher bearers and their burden all fall to snipers in about 20 seconds. When I reached the beach there were hundreds waiting to be attended to and all the time the bullets and shrapnel were flying about. Many were hit but by this time I didn't care whether they got me or not.

[Corporal William Rusden, New Zealand Expeditionary Force]

TOP LEFT: French soldier carrying his wounded comrade. (AWM G00470).

TOP RIGHT: The original grave of Private John Simpson Kirkpatrick, 3rd Australian Field Ambulance, Hell Spit Cemetery, Anzac. (AWM C02207).

LEFT: Private John Simpson Kirkpatrick, 3rd Australian Field Ambulance, who became famous for carrying wounded soldiers from the firing lines on a donkey. He was killed on 19 May 1915. (AWM J063920).

*There came a day when 'Murphy's Mules' came not. Stretcher bearers were working overtime, and the wounded cried 'For God's sake, send Murphy's mules!' Later on they found the mules grazing contentedly in Shrapnel valley. Then they found poor 'Murphy' ... He had done his last journey to the top of the hill. 'Where's Murphy?' demanded one of the 1st Battalion. 'Murphy's at heaven's gate,' answered the sergeant, 'helping the soldiers through'.*

[Major Oliver Hogue, 6th Light Horse Regiment, AIF]

*The condition of the wounded is indescribable. They lie in the sand in rows upon rows, their faces caked with sand and blood; one murmurs for water; no shelter from the sun; many of them in saps, with men passing all the time scattering more dust on them. There is hardly any possibility of transporting them. The fire zones are desperate and the saps are blocked with ammunition transport and mules, also whinnying for water, carrying food, etc. Some unwounded men also mad from thirst, cursing.*

[Aubrey Herbert, British Intelligence Officer, Anzac Corps]

RIGHT: A surgeon of a British Field Ambulance of the 42nd East Lancashire Division operating in the open air behind the firing line at Hellas. (AWM G00302).

FAR RIGHT: Dressing station, Brighton Beach, Anzac. (AWM H00252).

LEFT: Men of the 4th Australian Field Ambulance tending wounded soldiers lying in the open on stretchers at Walden Grove, Gallipoli, 7 August 1915. The photograph was probably taken by Alexander Hood, 4th Field Ambulance, and he wrote on it 'No tents, no blankets, damn little tucker — it was over this work that I was mentioned in dispatches'. (AWM P01116.064).

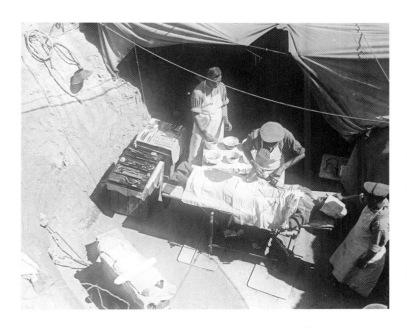

Lieutenant-Colonel H R Varker, 1/1st East Lancashire Field Ambulance, dressing the wounds of a Turkish prisoner, Helles. (AWM G00244).

*The condition of the men of the battalion was awful. Thin, haggard, as weak as kittens and covered with suppurating sores. The total strength of the battalion was two officers and 170 men. If we had been in France the men would have been sent to hospital.*

[Regimental Medical Officer, 15th Battalion, AIF]

A wounded soldier being transferred onto a hospital ship.

TOP RIGHT: Another method of bringing the wounded on board a hospital ship. (AWM C02277).

RIGHT: *After a Battle in Gallipoli*, from *The Sydney Mail*, 10 November 1915. This scene of barge-loads of wounded arriving at a hospital ship most likely occurred during evacuation from the battles of the 'August Offensive'. (NLA).

*In that terrible weather, with wind travelling a hundred miles an hour, and rain and sleet, all seems so pitifully hopeless ... During those fearful days our thoughts were constantly with the boys on the Peninsula and wondering how they were faring; but little did we realise the sufferings until the wind abated and they began to arrive with their poor feet and hands frostbitten. Thousands have been taken to Alexandria [Egypt], hundreds, the boys say, were drowned because their feet were so paralysed they could not crawl away to safety in time. They endured agonies. Sentries were found dead at their posts, frozen and still clutching their rifles ... their fingers were too frozen to pull the trigger. And some we have in hospital are losing both feet, some both hands. It's all too sad for words, hopelessly sad.*

[Sister Anne Donnell, Australian Army Nursing Service, AIF]

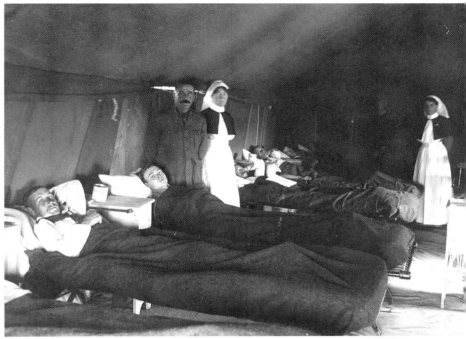

TOP: Interior of a ward at the 3rd Australian General Hospital, Lemnos Island. (SLNSW).

RIGHT: The 3rd Australian General Hospital, Lemnos Island, where the central walkway of this Sydney-raised unit was called 'Macquarie Street'. The hospital opened on 9 August 1915 during the 'August Offensive' and by 13 August it had over 800 patients. (SLNSW).

Wounded French soldiers homeward bound on a transport ship.
(AWM G00348).

RIGHT: A frost-bitten British soldier being helped into a lorry. Between 27 and 29 November 1915, severe storms, followed by freezing blizzards, hit Gallipoli. At Suvla there were 12,000 cases of frostbite and exposure, 3,000 at Anzac and 1,000 at Helles. (AWM G00652).

*On the 30th, when I made him [Hastabir Pun] show me his feet, to my horror I found them black with gangrene from neglected frostbite. He had never said a word to me and never would have. His case is not an exceptional one, but merely a typical example of the courage these Gurkhas displayed.*

[Captain Watson Smith, 1/6th Gurkha Rifles, British India Army]

*An Australian coastal holiday resort*

# BEACHES AND HARBOURS

One of the most visited locations on Gallipoli today is Anzac Cove. For years the annual Dawn Service was held at the Ari Burnu cemetery at the northern end of the cove, for it was around this point that some of the first waves of Australians came to shore on 25 April 1915. Anzac Cove has become one of the iconic images of the whole campaign.

Charles Bean described Anzac Cove as 'the complete base for an Army'. The beaches with their jetties and the man-made harbours were the lifelines of the allied forces on the peninsula. On or near the beaches grew those familiar tall and neat piles of wooden boxes and other stores and equipment that are such a feature of contemporary photographs. The beaches were also places where men from the front lines came to swim, scavenge, pick up stores, talk and gossip. From the beaches went forth rumours, 'furphies' and 'beachies' started often — or so it was asserted by the historian of the 28th Battalion — by the Intelligence Section of the General Staff!

But the beaches, like all parts of Gallipoli, were dangerous. From the day of the landing until the evacuation, the Turkish artillery regularly shelled Anzac Cove and the adjacent sea approaches. It probably helped morale among those who were exposed to the daily risks of the trenches that their senior commanders and headquarters staff, who lived and worked in dugouts behind the beaches, also ran the risk of being killed or maimed.

*Once more on old Anzac. What a change! Why, when we left there was hardly anything round this side of the Cove. It was not safe. Now there are tents and a YMCA and what is this great sandbag mansion going up directly in front of us? A Post Office, eh. Eighty feet long, twelve feet high and twenty-four feet wide. Some building! Windows, doors and a counter, too. Crikey, they are coming on in these parts.*

[Sergeant Cyril Lawrence, 2nd Field Company, Engineers AIF

The Sphinx towering over the Army Service Corps depot, North Beach. (AWM P00061.004).

TOP LEFT: The harbour at Suvla Bay on the afternoon before the final evacuation, 19 December 1915. This facility was built and maintained by men of the Royal Australian Navy Bridging Train. (AWM H12312).

BOTTOM LEFT: After the 'August Offensive', North Beach was developed as a main supply site for the Anzac position. An immense quantity of supplies was gathered here beneath the Sphinx at the Army Service Corps depot, and from early November the 1st Australian Stationary Hospital was also located at North Beach. (AWM A02854).

*ANZAC*, from *The Sydney Mail*, 20 October 1915. The beach at Anzac Cove, with its piers and piled boxes of stores, was an image strongly associated in the popular mind with the Australians at Gallipoli. (NLA).

Looking inland at Anzac Cove during a storm. (AWM A02703).

RIGHT: Turkish prisoners awaiting embarkation from Watson's Pier, Anzac Cove, 9 August 1915. Notice the forage for the mules and horses. (AWM J02391).

*When the struggle of the Landing had subsided, the Beach on summer days reminded many onlookers of an Australian coastal holiday resort ... on the hillside the little tracks winding through the low scrub, irresistibly recalled the Manly of New South Wales or the Victorian Sorrento, while the sleepy 'tick-tock' of rifles from behind the hills suggested the assiduous practice of batsmen at their nets on some neighbouring cricket field.*

[Charles Bean, official Australian war historian]

*Australians at Anzac*, from *The Sydney Mail*, 20 October 1915. Part of the caption reads: 'In the foreground are men with rifles returning from the firing line, while Field Ambulance men are starting off to the trenches with medical supplies. All over the hill are dug-outs, some of which have calico or canvas coverings, and men may be seen engaged in various duties.' (NLA).

*Bathing to the Accompaniment of Bursting Shells*, from *The Sydney Mail*, 19 May 1915. This was the first illustration showing the Australians on Gallipoli in *The Sydney Mail*. The artist based his scene on the recently published account — 8 May 1915 — of the landing by English journalist Ellis Ashmead Bartlett. The caption reads in part: 'These colonials are extraordinarily cool under fire, often exposing themselves rather than take the trouble to keep under shelter of the cliff. One of the strangest sights was to see men bathing in the sea with shrapnel bursting all round them.' (NLA).

Australian soldiers trying to salvage stores during an autumn storm. These storms caused great damage at Anzac Cove and they were one of the reasons for the build-up of the comparatively safe depot at North Beach. (AWM C01628).

*At 5 pm, on the day of the storm, all hands and the cook were summoned to Anzac Cove. On arrival it was found that the piers had been washed away. Big baulks of timber were being thrown about by the sea, in a most disconcerting manner, amongst all sorts of stores. The first duty assigned to the party by the Beach Commander was to restore some semblance of order amongst the members of a certain Labour Corps who had run wild. This was done in an expeditious though somewhat violent manner. The next duty was salvaging amongst the flotsam and jetsam which, with the timber charging about and the water at a very low temperature, was a decidedly unpleasant task. Night put a stop to the operations, and the Beach Commander congratulated the party on the work done. This officer was no lover of the 'Aussies', owing — so rumour had it — to some of them 'pinching' his fattening fowls, but on this occasion he contributed voluntarily to a double issue of rum, an act which was undoubtedly popular and timely.*

[Colonel H B Collett, 28th Battlion, AIF]

The British harbour at Lancashire Landing, Helles. Constructed of partly sunken ships, this was a far more elaborate affair than the cruder facilities at Anzac and Suvla. (AWM H10337).

*Long Weary Months*
# DAILY LIFE

As Charles Bean points out in one of his dispatches from Gallipoli, the life of a infantry soldier consisted of short bursts of 'frantic activity' — battle — followed by 'weary months' of digging, fetching and carrying. To these duties the Army gave the appropriate title of 'fatigues'. At Anzac, men were undoubtedly fatigued by the endless need to carry water and other materials from supply points up into steep and lofty places unreachable by the mules of the Indian Mule Cart Transport.

Gallipoli was not just about staying alive and unharmed. Each day was a struggle to eat as well as possible, to keep clean and to make life tolerable under extraordinary circumstances.

Unlike the French, who were able to establish somewhat elaborate field kitchens because of the nature of the terrain behind their positions at Helles, the men on the Anzac front lines had to do much of the cooking themselves from provisions obtained from battalion quartermasters. The quality of the food was a constant complaint as meals often consisted of monotonous portions of hard biscuits, jam, bully beef and tea. Efforts were made to supply the men with meat, bread, and vegetables but veteran memory of Gallipoli is all about the uniformly awful nature of the diet.

To keep clean, a man had to save up enough water from his ration to have a full body wash — the only alternative being the occasional visit to the beach. Hygiene in the trenches and back areas became a major problem and, as a result of the bad diet and fly-spread disease, many more men were evacuated sick from the peninsula than were killed or wounded by the enemy. For example, during August, September and October, out of 94,000 evacuations from the British Empire armies on Gallipoli, 57,000 were sick and 36,800 were wounded.

Turkish prisoners were often used for hard labour and one of the more poignant images of Gallipoli is that of two Turkish soldiers beside a row of graves they have just dug for French dead.

Life, however, also had its quieter moments such as during a church service, keeping up with paperwork or the reading of a letter from home.

*The French got a daily ration of red wine, and I think that after most of the officers of our mess gave up their ration of lime juice and drank red wine, obtained from the French headquarters, their health improved.*

[Major General W G Birrell, Director Medical Services, Mediterranean Expeditionary Force]

TOP: Wine on its way to the French troops at Helles. (AWM G00397).

RIGHT: A shipment of 'hard-tack' biscuits on its way to Gallipoli. (AWM G00203).

FAR RIGHT: *Each One Doing His Bit*, (with bread coming in a distant last), by Otho Hewett, from *The Anzac Book*. (AWM).

EACH ONE DOING HIS BIT

*Drawn by W. OTHO HEWETT*

DAILY LIFE

83

A kitchen in the snow, White Gully,
Anzac, 29 November 1915. (AWM G00126).

*But Oh, Hindus and Mussulmans, and Sikhs of Hindustan, just think for a moment. Why have you come here? And why are you wasting and ruining your lives here? Why are you dying from the swords and rifles of the Turks, with whom you have no quarrel, widowing your wives and orphaning your children? What benefit will there be to you or to your children, to your country, or to your people from your dying here? None whatever!*

[Section of Turkish leaflet thrown into the Indian lines at Gallipoli]

Ghurka soldiers from Nepal cooking at Walden Grove, Anzac, August 1915. Three battalions of the Ghurka Rifles fought with the Anzac Corps from mid-August 1915. (AWM C00681).

*There have been several great days at Anzac; the first was the day we landed, the second the day we got bacon for breakfast, the third the day we got bread, and the fourth the day we got news.*

[Charles Bean, official dispatch]

*There is an appetising crowing of roosters over to the north-east in some Turkish farmyard. I can hear the dogs barking too. It sounds as peaceful as a west Australian holding.*

[Captain Ferdinand Medcalf, 11th Battalion, AIF]

RIGHT: Early morning tea, Suvla. (AWM G00588).

FAR LEFT: An officers' mess of the British Naval Brigade Field Ambulance. (AWM PS1689).

TOP LEFT: British soldier warming up his dinner. (AWM G00297).

BOTTOM LEFT: Officers of the Royal Naval Division, Helles, with their chickens. (AWM G006180).

*We had porridge and treacle for breakfast this morning and milk, MILK, mind you. Yes. Golly, just fancy, condensed MILK. Jingo, if only some of those at home, who perhaps grumbled at their breakfast because the toast was cold, if only they knew what this little extra means to us, they would blush for shame and rightly so. Here they, like us, would eat anything.*

[Sergeant Cyril Lawrence, 2nd Field Company, Engineers, AIF]

DAILY LIFE

Greeks ferrying goats and sheep ashore at Gallipoli for the Indian troops. (AWM A02037).

BOTTOM: A British soldier with a fish killed by a shell from a Turkish gun nicknamed 'Asiatic Annie'. When it was found that shells exploding in the water killed fish, bombs were used surreptitiously for this purpose to help vary the monotonous army rations. (AWM G00329).

> We were very lucky today, in getting fresh fish, these fish are got by bombs, the concussion temporarily stuns them and you just wade into the sea and pick them up.
>
> [Private Victor Laidlaw, 2nd Australian Field Ambulance, AIF]

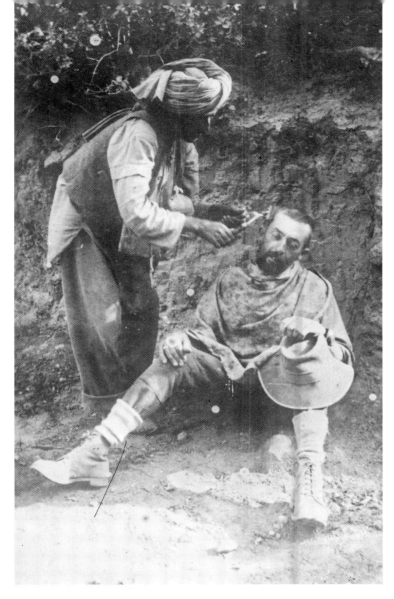

The Anzacs called every Indian 'Johnny' and treated him like a brother, with the consequences that the Indians liked them even more ... I often saw parties of Australians and New Zealanders sitting in the lines, eating chupatties and talking to the men.

[Major H M Alexander, Indian Mule Transport]

*Anzac Fashions: Winter*, by Bombadier Arthur Scott, Australian Field Artillery, from *The Anzac Book*. (AWM).

LEFT: An Indian soldier cutting an Australian's hair with horse clippers, Anzac, August 1915. (AWM C01139).

*Papers were what we needed most. I wrote home once that I was fortunate in having a paper to read that had been wrapped round a piece of greasy bacon … We were up the gully at the advance dressing station, and a machine gun was playing right down the position. Four men were killed and six wounded right in front of us, so that it was not prudent to leave until night fell. It was then that reading matter became so necessary. The paper was the* Sydney Morning Herald *and contained an advertisement stating that there was a vacancy for two boarders at Katoomba. I was an applicant for the vacancy. The* Bulletin *was a God-send when it arrived, as was* Punch. *Norman Morris occasionally got files of the* Newcastle Morning Herald, *which he would hand on to us as there were a lot of men from Newcastle district in the Ambulance. Later it was possible to register a small parcel in the Field Post Office — for home.*

[Joseph Beeston, 4th Field Ambulance, AIF]

TOP: Officers of the Lancashire Fusiliers reading the *Tatler*, a well-known British illustrated magazine, Helles. (AWM G00343).

LEFT: Queenslanders of the 7th Battery, Australian Field Artillery, relaxing in the Lone Pine area. The man on the left is reading *The Sphere*, a popular London magazine. (AWM H03547).

## Advertisements

### PUBLIC NOTICES

NOTICE.—The Turkish artillery is requested to refrain from wasting ammunition whilst our meals are being served.

PUBLIC NOTICE.—The Electric Elevator will not be working up the gullies for a while. Some cook stole the current to make a pudding.

KABA TEPE MUSEUM.—Come and see! A piece of long extinct Australian butter now being exhibited.
*Admission.*—One slice of bread.

BENEVOLENT HOME.—The Editor has established a home for lost newspapers and books. Any books or papers may be left there and no questions asked.

MEDICAL.—Men suffering from a feeling of fullness after eating, are requested to state where they got the extra rations from.

WARNING.—Men are advised to keep their eyes open for an individual wearing pink pyjamas, green glasses, straw hat and khaki mackintosh. It is thought that this is a spy in disguise.

### PERSONAL, MISSING FRIENDS, etc.

LAST seen two months ago in Scotland, at the Duke of Buckington's grouse shoot. Pte. Bert Backblocks. Left Gallipoli with serious wound in fingernail early in May. Any information as to present whereabouts of above will be gratefully received by Adjutant, 101st Battn.

CHARLIE.—Come back, dearest. A warm welcome is prepared for you. Loving arms will enfold you.—Serg.-Maj. Bawler.

OH how we missed you, dearest Bill,
  On that famed August nine,
We think about you, Billie, still
  In Cairo drinking wine.

MISSING.—A little tot. It's rum where it's got to.

MISSING FRIENDS, ETC.—Will the girl who smiled at William Tomkins last Boxing Day please write to him at once?

LOST BY A POOR PERSON.—A strong pipe, last smelt in someone's pocket up Monash Gully.

LOST.—Pair of field glasses. Finder please return same to our Champion Optimist.

### WANTED

WANTED.—The address of a good barber. One able to cut hair and shave preferred. Apply any platoon.

WANTED.—Section commander requires pair of good field glasses to find his men when there is shrapnel about.

Q.M.S. requires a man who can even partly satisfy mess orderlies.

EXCHANGE.—Corporal would exchange a wristlet watch (not going) for a spring mattress or a tin of MacConochie's Rations.

WANTED.—Some nice girls to stroll with on the Engineers' North Pier.

WANTED.—Fifty thousand Turkish prisoners for wharf-lumping, road-making, and building officers' dugouts. Plenty of permanent work for men of right stamp. Apply any beach fatigue party—Australian N. Z. Army Corps.

FULL private wishes to buy guide book to London. Places safe from Zeppelin to be marked with a cross.

TO LET.—Nice dugout on the skyline. Owner leaving for field hospital.

### MISCELLANEOUS

MAN with good memory would like the job of taking messages from the troops to friends in Cairo.

WANTED TO BUY.—The 2nd Brigade will buy large or small quantities of old beer. Fresh beer not objected to.

READ Prof. Fire Trench's book on the killing of insect pests with a shovel.

BUSINESS FOR SALE.—Mess orderly will sell goodwill of a flourishing business for a box of fags.

COMPLETE SPY OUTFIT FOR SALE.— Including pair of blucher boots, sombrero hat, two cutlasses and a yashmak. Owner having failed to be discovered for two days is going out of business.
  Sergt. Noonan, 6th Battn.

165

Resting in the trenches, Anzac. (AWM PS1517).

LEFT: Humorous advertisements from *The Anzac Book*, written and illustrated on Gallipoli, and published in 1916. The editor of *The Anzac Book*, Charles Bean, wrote: 'The book of ANZAC was produced in the lines of Anzac at Gallipoli in the closing weeks of 1915. Practically every word was written beneath a waterproof sheet or under a roof of sandbags either in the trenches or within the range of a Turkish rifle'. (AWM).

An open-air communion service, Anzac. (AWM G01432).

*The padres and their congregations are not immune from shelling. This morning during a simple church service ... a 6-inch or 8-inch shell came over and exploded not so far away — just on the other side of the valley, to be exact in the midst of eight men. The shell raised an enormous dust: none of the men were hurt. The padre continued his sermon exactly as if he had been in church, and a bird had flown in the window, while the congregation, like a lot of schoolboys, all turned round to see what had been the effect of the shell.*

[Charles Bean, official dispatch]

Mail being distributed to the 1st Australian Light Horse Field Ambulance, Chailak Dere, Anzac. (AWM C03613).

LEFT: Lieutenant Colonel Carew Reynell, Commanding Officer, 9th Australian Light Horse Regiment, 'chatting' — picking lice from his clothing — 27 August 1915. Reynell was killed in action the following day. (AWM H02784).

Private Morrow bathing outside his dugout at Chailak Dere, Anzac. (AWM C03611).

RIGHT: Staff Sergeant Lionel Sargent, 4th Australian Field Ambulance, doing his washing. (AWM P1116.69.62).

*Occasionally in the line there was a cool spell, and a man might have saved enough water from his daily ration to collect a pint or two in order to get a shave or the substitute for a wash.*

[Captain Walter Belford, 11th Battalion, AIF]

Christmas mail for Sergeant Clark, 7th Australian Field Ambulance, December 1915. (AWM H00294).

FAR LEFT: Members of 4th Australian Field Ambulance with their Christmas billies. The billies came from the Australian Red Cross and included a variety of Christmas treats. (AWM P01116.024).

*We received our Xmas billies on the 22nd [December 1915] and very good they were. On the outside of the billy cans they had a kangaroo with his feet on Anzac and underneath were the words 'This bit of the world belongs to us'. That caused many a laugh for we had sneaked away from it. They made a mess of the billy cans for we got the Victorians and they got ours.*

[Private Archie Barwick, 1st Battalion, AIF]

DAILY LIFE

95

*Sand makes a poor road. To get a reasonable result it was necessary to collect the big stones of the seashore and carry them to the shore edge of the beach and place them as a foundation; on the top of this clay was deposited ... the whole area was top-dressed by the sand of the beach and finally the hard-worked soldiers carried petrol tins of water from the sea and poured it over the surface to make the material set. So, harassed by the splutter of machine guns night after night, and weakened by the heat of the day, the faithful souls of the working parties steadily carried the road from Anzac Cove along North Beach towards the Suvla flats.*

[Major Fred Waite, New Zealand Expeditionary Force]

LEFT: Road-making in the valley behind Destroyer Hill, Anzac. (AWM A00903).

RIGHT: Australian water carriers, Victoria Gully, Anzac, August 1915. (AWM C01451).

*You must not imagine that life in one of these modern battles consists of continuous bomb fighting, bayonetting and bombarding all the time. These 'progresses', 'consolidatings', 'bomb-droppings', 'artillery activity', of the war reports are the incidents in long, weary months, whose chief occupation is the digging of mile upon mile of endless sap [trench] of sunken road, through which troops and mules can pass safely ... The carrying of biscuit boxes and building timbers for hours daily, the waiting in weary queues, of thirty half-dry wells, for the privilege of carrying endless water cans for half a mile uphill ... the sweeping and disinfecting of trenches in the never ending fight against flies — this is the soldiers life for nine days out of ten in a modern battle. War consists of a long series of what seems at the time to be endless delays, interspersed by short bursts of frantic activity.*

[Charles Bean, official dispatch]

Australians and Maoris dragging a water tank up to a terrace beneath Plugge's Plateau, Anzac. (AWM C01812).

BOTTOM LEFT: British Army Ordnance Corps soldiers cleaning and fumigating uniforms. (AWM H10316).

BOTTOM RIGHT: British and Australian soldiers driving in a flock of sheep for butchering. (AWM G00441).

A French field kitchen within half a kilometre of the Turkish lines, Helles. (AWM G00478).

LEFT: Major Dennis King, 1st Infantry Brigade headquarters, doing paperwork, Anzac, December 1915. (AWM J02559).

We have a clerk here, Venables. He has got tired of writing, and wanting to change the pen for the sword, borrowed a rifle and walked up to the front line at Quinn's Post. There he popped his head in and said: 'Excuse me, is this a private trench, or may anyone fire out of it.

[Aubrey Herbert, British Intelligence Officer, Anzac Corps]

DAILY LIFE

99

Field bakery, Turk's Head Peninsula, Lemnos Island, December 1915. (AWM C1198).

*The daily supply [of bread] was at first towed from Imbros to Anzac in a barge; but since these consignments were always held up by any freshness in the wind, the bread was eventually carried in a trawler, which sailed almost daily from Imbros. Shortage of the Imbros water-supply constantly interrupted the baking, and fuel was difficult to obtain, grass being used on at least one occasion. Shipments of wood were eventually obtained from a Greek contractor named Goulandris, who brought them — partly from Mt. Athos — at £2 2s. a ton. Until the end of July the rations to Anzac, daily supplied G.H.Q. [General Headquarters] and any troops on the island. At this stage numerous bakeries arrived, all of which were placed under Captain Prior's [Commander, 1st Australian Field Bakery] command until by August 30 he had, besides his own, the 10th, 11th, 29th, 50th and 51st Divisional Bakeries, though most of these were at first handicapped through being unaccustomed to brew their own yeast. After August the daily supply was normally — to Anzac, 20,000 rations; to Suvla — 40,000 rations.*

[Charles Bean, official Australian war historian.]

Turkish prisoners digging graves, Helles. (AWM G00485).

RIGHT: Dispatch riders of the British Royal Engineers (Signal Service), Helles. (AWM G00385).

Lieutenant Stanley Watson (right) 1st Division Signal Company, supervising the building of Watson's Pier, Anzac Cove, June 1915. (AWM G01046).

The 5th Light Horse Brigade's butcher's shop, Anzac. (AWM P02023.005).

BOTTOM: Civilian workmen employed in the Dardanelles area waiting for a boat to take them to their worksite. (AWM H10303).

*I don't know what we would have done without the mules at Anzac. I reckon we would have starved you should have seen some of the tracks they had to climb and talk about slippery, every bit of food, ammunition, clothing and nearly all our water had to be carried by the mule teams up to the trenches it was a task I can tell you and it had practically all to be done at night time for the Turks could see them in daylight. The Indians were responsible for all this work and deserve a heap of praise, there were a good few of them chaps killed at Anzac.*

[Private Archie Barwick, 1st Battalion, AIF]

TOP: An Indian mule cart and driver, North Beach, Anzac. (AWM C01635).

LEFT: Donkeys carrying water in recycled petrol tins, North Beach, Anzac.

DAILY LIFE

*A perfectly comfortable habitation*

# DWELLINGS

Visitors to the Anzac position on Gallipoli during 1915 felt it to be one of the strangest looking communities even seen. English journalist Henry Nevinson wrote of how the Anzacs stared out at the sea from the 'mouths of little caves cut in the face of the cliffs'. This phrase neatly describes the dwellings of the ordinary soldiers at Anzac. Often these were holes or 'dugouts' covered with a canopy of scrub held up by pieces of wood or with whatever protection against the elements they could find. *The Sydney Mail* published many shots of these primitive residences and tried to reassure anxious families in Australia that by burrowing into the earth their sons and husbands were safe from Turkish shrapnel. They further suggested that the troops were able to make themselves 'comfortable in these subterranean shelters'.

The nature of this shelter varied depending whether it was in the front lines or in a back area. In the trenches men made do with scrape holes hollowed out of the trench wall or simply slept on the ground. In reserve, just behind the line, covered 'dugouts' were constructed into the sides of even the most precipitous slopes. Further back, headquarters staffs were accommodated in slightly more elaborate structures that were sometimes protected by sandbags. In many instances soldiers did what they could to soften their surroundings by pinning up photographs and even pages from newspapers.

A British soldier in his dugout, West Beach, Sedd-el-Bahr, Helles. (AWM G00768).

LEFT: New Zealand troops resting in the trenches on Rhododendron Spur, Anzac, a few weeks after it was taken, September 1915. (AWM G01217).

*A few had 'bivvies' excavated in the walls of the trenches, but most men had only the floor of the trench upon which to lie. Here, clothed in their overcoats and wrapped in their single blankets, they slumbered — only to be rudely awakened now and then by the pressure on some part of their anatomy of the feet of a passenger to or from the front line ... In the front trenches, where the garrisons were relieved by the supports every 24 hours, sleep was, theoretically, not to be thought of. However, the normal man felt that at some time during the 24 hours it was good to close his tired eyes — if only for a few minutes.*

[Colonel Herbert Collett, 28th Battalion, AIF]

Lieutenant Colonel Arthur Bauchop, Commanding Officer, Otago Mounted Rifles, NZEF, in front of his living quarters, No 2 Outpost, North Beach, Anzac. His hut was partly constructed from the oars of the boats of 7th Battalion, AIF, which were stranded near the site of the outpost on 25 April 1915. (AWM G00983-A02031).

LEFT: This position, on the seaward slopes at Steele's Post, was held by a detachment of the 1st Battalion, AIF, from 3 May 1915, despite Turkish snipers having reached the gully opposite during the first week of the occupation. (AWM G00942).

*The mess dugout, in which I also slept, was made very comfortable and quite proof against splinters and bullets ... The earth was dug to a depth of about three feet: walls were made of grain-bags filled with sand, a large biscuit-box, with top and bottom knocked off, forming a good window on the west side. A roof was put on, strips of wood collected from the wreckage of a boat being used as rafters, with a cart tarpaulin stretched over them, and two inches of earth on top. The whole south side above the ground line was left open to give a splendid view across the position to Ari Burnu Point, and Imbros Island behind. The furniture consisted of shelves and cupboards of biscuit-boxes, a tarpaulin on the floor, a large-size bully-beef box as a table, a most luxurious camp-chair contributed by Hashmet Ali, and two stools cleverly made by the Corps carpenter from odds and ends. My valise on a layer of hay was the bed, and when rolled up was used as a fourth chair. The open side was fitted with curtains made of ration-bags, which could be let down to keep out the afternoon sun. It was a perfectly comfortable habitation, though a little cramped at times. The dimensions were not more than seven feet long and five feet wide, and about four feet deep.*

[Major H M Alexander, Indian Mule Transport]

FAR LEFT: British Army soldier writing a letter in his dugout in the side of a cliff, Helles. The steps were made from sand bags. (AWM H10323).

LEFT: A British sailor on shore duty at Anzac resting in his dugout near the beach. (AWM C00815).

BOTTOM: Steps cut into the hillside behind Pope's Post, Anzac, strengthened with packing cases. (AWM H15375).

LEFT: Drawing lampooning the living conditions on Gallipoli, contributed to *The Anzac Book* by Captain Leslie Hore, 8th Light Horse Regiment, 1915. (AWM).

BOTTOM: Rows of substantial dugouts on the slopes above the beach, Anzac. (AWM P0437.92.11).

DWELLINGS

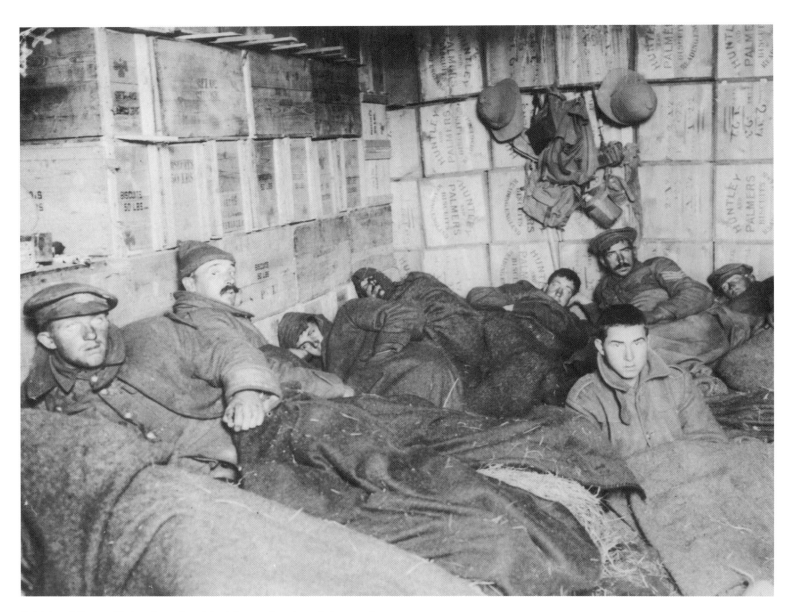

British soldiers suffering from frostbite lying on hay in a shelter made of boxes of stores. (AWM H10373).

Hospital tents from 4th Australian Field Ambulance under snow in Hotchkiss Gully after the blizzards of November 1915. Hotchkiss Gully lay in steep hills at the northern end of the Anzac position. (AWM C00680).

RIGHT: A British official photograph of a soldier visiting his comrade's grave on the cliffs, Cape Helles. (AWM G00363).

BOTTOM LEFT: This illustration – *The Battle of Lone Pine on 400 Plateau, near Anzac – A Great Australian Feat* – was published in the *London Illustrated News*, 25 September 1915. (AWM PS2704).

BOTTOM RIGHT: Cover of *The Sydney Mail: War Issue No LIV*, 11 August 1915. (NLA).

*The Trembling Sultan*, from *The Sydney Mail*, 22 September 1915. Mohammed V was the Sultan of Turkey at the time Gallipoli campaign. (NLA).

LEFT: Staff Sergeant Arthur Pascall, 4th Field Ambulance, in his tent, Hotchkiss Gully, Anzac. On the walls behind him are a number of images published in illustrated British and Australian newspapers during 1915, particularly *The Sydney Mail* and which are also shown on these pages. (AWM C00678).

*You can't leave it*

# EVACUATION

On the night of 19–20 December 1915 the last Australian, New Zealand and British troops left the Anzac and Suvla positions. On 8–9 January 1916 the British evacuated Helles: the French had already left. Both operations proved to be the most successful part of the whole campaign and there were virtually no casualties. At Anzac, as a result of various carefully staged subterfuges, the Turks seemed to have been unaware right to the end that the Anzacs were pulling out.

Basically, the allies admitted defeat, accepting that there was little likelihood that they could break through the Turkish resistance with the resources they were prepared to commit to Gallipoli. Also, at Anzac there had been great concern about the problems of supplying thousands of men throughout the stormy winter months — particularly since they were so dependent on the flimsy jetties of Anzac Cove and North Beach.

For the men of the AIF, the evacuation brought mixed emotions. Everyone wanted to be among the last to go. What bit most deeply into their souls was having to leave their dead uncared for in the cemeteries which were now to be found all over the Anzac position. Bean observed how many men were to be seen tending and visiting the graves. As he waited to embark on 19 December, Company Quarter Master Sergeant Alfred Guppy, 14th Battalion, wrote:

*Sleep sound, old friends – the keenest part*
*Which, more than failure, wounds the heart,*
*Is thus to leave you – thus to part.*

British soldiers preparing stores for incineration before the evacuation of Anzac and Suvla. (AWM G00639).

*I came down — I got off my perch (the firing step) ... I walked through the trench and the floor of the trench was frozen hard ... and when I brought my feet down they echoed right through the trench, down the gully, right down, and you could hear this echo running ahead ... Talk about empty, I didn't see a soul ... It was a lonely feeling.*

[Company Sergeant Major Joe Gasparich, Auckland Infantry Battalion, New Zealand Expeditionary Force]

*How can they leave this place? Ours, because it is ours and ours alone: we fought for it and won it; even leaving that out of the account, just think of all it means, the leaving of this place. It has grown upon one: we took it, and tamed it and somehow its very wildness and ruggedness grips you. You can't leave it.*

[Sergeant Cyril Lawrence, 2nd Field Company, Engineers, AIF]

A Royal Navy steam launch towing a raft carrying British Army artillerymen and their guns out to waiting ships before the evacuation, Suvla Bay, December 1915. (AWM H10385).

RIGHT: Dummy soldiers used to convince the Turks that the Helles garrison was being maintained, just prior to its evacuation on 8–9 January 1916. (AWM Bastion Collection A77).

*An enormous amount of war stores of every kind had been left behind by the English in their retirement. In the space from Suvla Bay to Ari Burnu five smaller steamers and over sixty boats were left on the beach. Narrow-gauge railways, telephone stores, barbed-wire and entanglement material in very great quantities, also heaps of tools of every sort, dispensaries, many medical stores and drinking-water clarifiers were found. A great quantity of artillery and infantry ammunition, also whole rows of wagons and limbers, had been left behind, likewise small arms of every sort, chests of hand-grenades, and machine-gun barrels. Many dumps of tinned rations, flour, provisions and piles of wood were found. The complete camp tentage of the enemy had been left standing and was sacrificed! ... Several hundred horses, which had not been able to be embarked, lay dead in long rows.*

[Liman von Sanders, German commander of the Turkish armies on Gallipoli]

FAR LEFT: An Australian soldier, 'Doc' Cherry, with his equipment and belongings on the day of his evacuation from Anzac, December 1915. (AWM P176.20.17).

LEFT: The British fleet leaving Kephalos Harbour, Imbros Island, for the final evacuation of Anzac and Suvla, 19 December 1915. (AWM G01442L).

BOTTOM: Turkish officers watching the Allied ships withdrawing from the Gallipoli peninsula, December 1915. (AWM A05297).

RIGHT: *So Long Turkey, Will See You Later*, cartoon drawn by Hal Eyre in 1915 for the Sydney *Daily Telegraph*. (SLNSW).

# GALLIPOLI PORTRAITS

On Gallipoli, hundreds of soldiers were undoubtedly asked to face the photographer and smile. Others had their picture taken without being asked for any response. General William Birdwood, for example, as he swam at Anzac Cove, acknowledged that a camera was being pointed in his direction and he gazed up out of the water towards it. And then there were the formal group shots where everyone was arranged as speedily and artistically as possible — tallest to the back, ladies to the middle. How many photographs, taken on Gallipoli, ended up in family albums? We will never know.

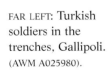

FAR LEFT: Turkish soldiers in the trenches, Gallipoli. (AWM A025980).

LEFT: Anzacs — Australians and New Zealanders — in the front line, Anzac. (AWM C03420).

Australians going for a swim, Lemnos Island. (AWM A01541).

TOP LEFT: Two patients outside the officers' ward relax with their gramophone, Lemnos Island, 1915. (AWM A05361).

LEFT: Staff of the operating theatre, 3rd Australian General Hospital, Lemnos Island. (AWM J01377).

Lieutenant Norman Holbrook VC, Royal Navy, commander of submarine B11, on board HMS *Adamant*, Dardanelles, 1915. (AWM G004530).

LEFT: Trooper Alan Huthwaite, 1st Australian Light Horse at No 1 Outpost, Anzac, August 1915. Huthwaite, aged 50 and described as 'an old soldier', died in Egypt in November 1917. (AWM C02735).

## *Tea on the Terrace*
# THE GALLIPOLI DRAWINGS OF CAPTAIN LESLIE HORE

Captain Leslie Hore, 8th Light Horse Regiment, AIF, spent five months with his unit on Gallipoli. During that time he produced and sent home 44 small drawings, mostly in watercolour or coloured pencil, giving his impressions of the campaign and the landscape of the peninsula.

In these drawings, and through the titles he gave some of them, Hore showed himself to be a sensitive and thoughtful observer of the tragedy and beauty of Gallipoli. The sorrow of war is evident in his portrayal of dead Turkish soldiers lying outside the trenches of the 8th Light Horse at Walker's Ridge on the morning of 30 June 1915. In the dark, the Turks had attacked the Light Horse forward positions, where Hore was in charge. The Turks, men of the 18th Regiment, were driven off with great loss and, as Bean wrote, 'daylight had found the men of this fine regiment scattered over those deadly heights'. It is the poignancy of these 'scattered' bodies that Hore captures in his drawing 'The Morning After – 30/VI/15'.

*Anzac Beach*, June 1915. Hore's rendition of Anzac Cove. (SLNSW).

But what is most striking about Hore's Gallipoli is the way he juxtaposed the beauty of the Gallipoli landscape and familiar domestic activities with the backdrop of conflict. This combination is evident in his drawing 'The Bacchante tolls the knell of parting day'. As the late autumn sun sets over the island of Imbros, a kneeling soldier brews his tea while the Royal Navy's cruiser, *Bacchante*, fires at the Turks.

Hore's drawings were sold to the Mitchell Library, State Library of New South Wales, by his wife shortly after the war.

*Tea on the Terrace*, June 1915. Hore captures a moment of evening quiet as the sun sinks behind the island of Samothrace. (SLNSW).

There was a magnificent sunset. They all are here — just simply glorious. I do wish I had a decent photo or something of them. Away about fifteen miles off our position are two mountainous islands, Imbros and Samothrace. The sun goes below the sea's horizon just off the northern end of the latter throwing them both, great jagged peaks, into silhouette on a crimson background. The sea is nearly always like oil and as the crimson path streams across the water the store ships, hospital ships, torpedo boats and mine sweepers stand out jet black. God, it's just magnificent.

[Sergeant Cyril Lawrence, 2nd Field Company Engineers, AIF]

*A breather on Walker's Ridge*, June 1915. The camp of the Indian Mule Cart Transport was just below the positions of Hore's unit, the 8th Light Horse Regiment, on Walker's Ridge, Anzac. (SLNSW).

*The morning after, 30/vi/15.* Turkish soldiers killed in a night attack on the front line positions of the 8th Light Horse Regiment, Walker's Ridge, Anzac. (SLNSW).

*His day's work done*, October 1915. (SLNSW).

On one occasion at Suvla a rough sea washed all the top of a burial ground away leaving the carcasses exposed. Some of the carcasses were towed out into the current from the Narrows; some of these were thus washed out into the sea, but the majority drifted in the current and were cast up on the beaches and rocks along the shore road, where they lay till broken up by the waves. At first the carcasses were not cut open and, after drifting out to sea, the hoofs projected out of the water and were on more than one occasion mistaken for the periscope of a hostile submarine.

[Major General Sir L J Blenkinsop and Lieutenant Colonel J W Rainey, official British war historians]

*The* Bacchante *tolls the knell of parting day*, November 1915. The *Bacchante*, a British cruiser, is in the central right of the drawing just below the island of Samothrace. It is firing at Turkish positions on Anzac. (SLNSW).

The cruiser Bacchante *was firing regularly at the flashes. Her shells were high explosive – that is to say, they hit the ground before they burst and depended for their effect upon the powerful explosive, which scattered abroad deadly fragments of the shell-case and tore great clouds of dust and earth from the neck [of land] upon which were the Turkish guns.*

[Charles Bean, official Australian war historian]

*The curfew tolls the knell of parting day,*
*The lowing herd wind slowly o'er the lea,*
*The plowman homeward plods his weary way,*
*And leaves the world to darkness and to me.*

[Thomas Gray, 'Elegy written in a Country Church-Yard']

*Frostbite*, December 1915. (SLNSW).

*Fame*, December 1915. (SLNSW).

*The most pathetic evidence that I have heard of Australian regard for the Turks is a little wooden cross found in the scrub, just two splinters of biscuit box tacked together, with the inscription 'Here lies a Turk'. The poor soul would probably turn in his grave if his ghost could see that rough cross above him. But he need not worry. It was put there in all sincerity. Some Australian found him and buried him exactly as he would bury one of our own men – with that last little homage to mark the resting-place of a man fighting for his country.*

[Charles Bean, official dispatch]

General Sir William Birdwood, commander, Anzac Corps, taking a dip. (AWM G00401).

LEFT: Lieutenant Oliver Hogue, 6th Light Horse Regiment, Anzac. Hogue was the author of *Trooper Bluegum at the Dardanelles*, a book of stories and poems about Anzac published in 1915. (AWM A02353).

RIGHT: Australian nurse from the 3rd Australian General Hospital leaving Lemnos Island with the unit mascot. (SLNSW).

BELOW: Soldier outside the 6th Field Ambulance dressing station, Wire Gully, Anzac. (AWM A01880).

132

TOP LEFT: A Turkish artilleryman lifting a 258 kilogram shell at one of the Dardanelles fortress batteries. (AWM A05301).

TOP RIGHT: A Maori soldier in the snow, Anzac, 30 November 1915. (AWM G01268).

LEFT: A Sergeant Major of the Indian Mule Transport, Anzac. (AWM P0229/13/04).

*Where our dead Australians lie*

# REMEMBERING GALLIPOLI

## 1915-1930

The landing at Gallipoli was quickly interpreted as a nation-building event for the young Commonwealth of Australia. Australian soldiers had stepped on to the world stage and, over a long and testing campaign, had shown themselves capable of endurance and of overcoming great loss. That loss was seen in the casualty figures — 8,700 dead and over 19,400 wounded. Total allied dead, including the French, came to over 44,000 with 97,000 wounded. Turkish deaths have been estimated at 86,000 with 164,000 wounded. Bean saw the Anzac area as 'one big graveyard'. He could equally have applied that phrase to the whole Gallipoli battlefield of 1915.

Well before the end of the campaign the word 'Anzac' entered the language. Bean wrote of the day of the landing as being the first Anzac Day and on 25 April 1916 the event was commemorated for the first time throughout Australia. Those who had been at Gallipoli and returned to Australia brought out picture books and souvenirs. As individuals and businesses pressed to use the word 'Anzac', the Commonwealth Government restricted its use for any but official commemorative purposes. A sad victim of this policy was Claude

Burton of Euroa, Victoria. He requested permission to name his house 'Anzac' in memory of his brother, Corporal Alexander Burton, 7th Battalion, AIF, who had been killed at the Battle of Lone Pine and had been awarded a posthumous Victoria Cross. Permission was refused by the Commonwealth Attorney General.

After World War I, the initial survey of the Anzac battlefield and eventually the construction of the allied cemeteries and memorials on the peninsula were undertaken, appropriately, by an Australian — Cyril Hughes. Hughes was an Anzac, having fought on Gallipoli in 1915. Today there are 32 allied cemeteries, 21 of which are in the Anzac area. Those cemeteries contain over 22,000 graves but only 9,000 contain identified remains. The names of those in the graves of the 'unknowns', and of those whose bodies were never found or were buried in the seas around the peninsula, are on memorials to the missing. Australia's memorial is at Lone Pine where fierce fighting took place during the Battles of the Landing (25 April-3 May 1915) and Lone Pine (7-9 August 1915). On a wall in front of the memorial are the names of the Australian missing, 4,228 of them, and on the memorial itself there are the names of 708 missing New Zealanders who fought and died there beside their Anzac comrades.

What happened on Gallipoli mattered very much to those who had served there. For years they gathered in their units on Anzac Day, or sometimes on other special days, to remember. What happened at Gallipoli still seems to matter, if the numbers now turning out for Anzac Day both in Australia and at Gallipoli are any guide. But perhaps the visitors that the Anzacs themselves would be most pleased to see are the younger ones who now make their way to Gallipoli for the Dawn Service. As Charles Bean knew, for as long as they keep going Anzac Day will have a future. Their very presence on Gallipoli at such a time gives continuing life and purpose to the lines of Anzac poet Lester Lawrence:

*Some flower that blooms beside the Southern foam*
*May blossom where our dead Australians lie,*
*And comfort them with whispers of their home:*
*And they will dream beneath the alien sky*
*Of the Pacific Sea.*

*For Valor!*, from *Melbourne Punch*, 10 June 1915. What is remarkable about this illustration is that it shows the speed with which the achievements of the Anzacs at Gallipoli were commemorated in Australia. (NLA).

## With the Anzacs at the Dardanelles.

J. & N. TAIT present
M R.
## ASHMEAD-BARTLETT
The world-famous War Correspondent.

## BOVRIL at the Front

"But for a plentiful supply of Bovril I don't know what we should have done. During Neuve Chapelle and other engagements we had big cauldrons going over log fires, and as we collected and brought in the wounded we gave each man a good drink of hot Bovril, and I cannot tell you how grateful they were."

Extract from letter from the Front.

### Fortify yourself with BOVRIL!

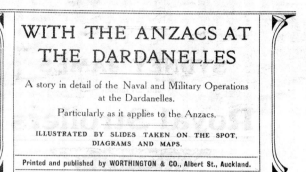

WITH THE ANZACS AT THE DARDANELLES

A story in detail of the Naval and Military Operations at the Dardanelles.

Particularly as it applies to the Anzacs.

ILLUSTRATED BY SLIDES TAKEN ON THE SPOT, DIAGRAMS AND MAPS.

Printed and published by WORTHINGTON & CO., Albert St., Auckland.

INSURE WITH
## The NEW ZEALAND
INSURANCE CO., LTD.

The PREMIER Colonial Company.

FIRE     MARINE     ACCIDENT
TRUSTEES AND EXECUTORS.

Cover of booklet and internal page of *With the Anzacs at the Dardanelles* advertising the lecture visit to New Zealand in March 1916 of British journalist Ellis Ashmead-Bartlett. Ashmead-Bartlett, who had been a war correspondent at Gallipoli, spent most of February, March and April 1916 lecturing about Gallipoli in Australia and New Zealand. (SLNSW).

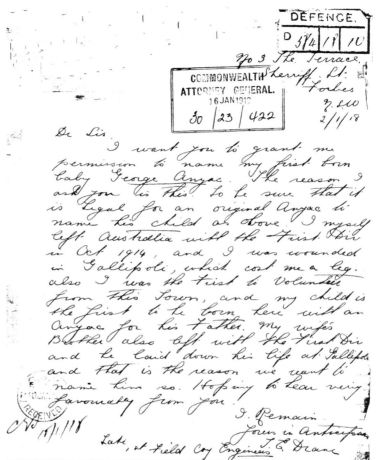

TOP: George Anzac Drane, 11 months. (Andrew Drane).

LEFT: Editorial from the *Daily Telegraph*, Sydney, 29 May 1916, supporting the decision by the Commonwealth Government to limit the use of the word 'Anzac'. (NAA).

In 1918, Gallipoli veteran Thomas Edward Drane, Forbes, New South Wales, wrote to the Commonwealth Attorney General asking for permission to name his first child 'George Anzac'. The Commonwealth Government claimed no powers in this area. (NAA. A432/86, 1929/3484 Pt.19).

LEFT: After he returned from Gallipoli, where he served with the 6th Battalion, AIF, James Molloy ran Lemos Lounge on Beach Road, Black Rock, Melbourne. He was, however, not allowed to advertise himself as 'late of Anzac'. (N.A. A432/86, 29/3484, Pt.11)

TOP RIGHT: In 1916, before the prohibition on the use of the word Anzac for commercial purposes, Lonsdale and Bartholomew, Melbourne, produced this 'Anzac' Christmas card. They were allowed to sell-off those they had already produced. (N.A. A432/86, 29/3484, Pt.17).

For Anzac Day 1917, Erine Mort, Sydney, drew this 'Wreath of eucalyptus boughs and leaves crossed vertically by a firebrand burning as a torch' for use by the Returned Soldiers' Association of New South Wales. (N.A. A1861/1, 3958).

> I beg to request that you [the Commonwealth Attorney General] will grant me permission to use the word 'Anzac' on my fruit barrow, for which I have been granted a stand in Wellington Street, Perth, immediately opposite the Central Railway Station by the Perth City Council. I may mention that I have served one year and forty-four days at the Dardanelles with the AIF 11th Battalion and have been invalided home with the endorsement on my discharge 'Conduct very good'. The word will in no sense be used as an advertisement, the quality and price of my fruit being their one and only recommendation, but is essential to have a distinct name on the barrow.
>
> [Frank Netherey, ex-11th Battalion, AIF, 1916]

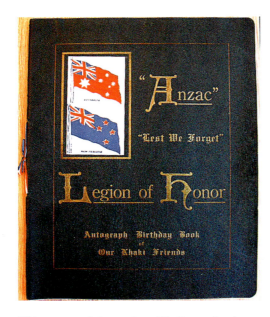

This proposed Anzac-Lest We Forget-Legion of Honour Autograph Birthday Book was submitted to the Attorney General but there is no indication in the records whether permission to publish was denied.
(NAA. A432/86, 29/3484 Pt.14).

RIGHT: In 1916, D Davis and Co., Sydney, were initially refused, but eventually permitted to use the word Anzac in the title of this march. General William Birdwood's picture was also part of the cover design.
(NAA. A432/86, 29/3484 Pt.14).

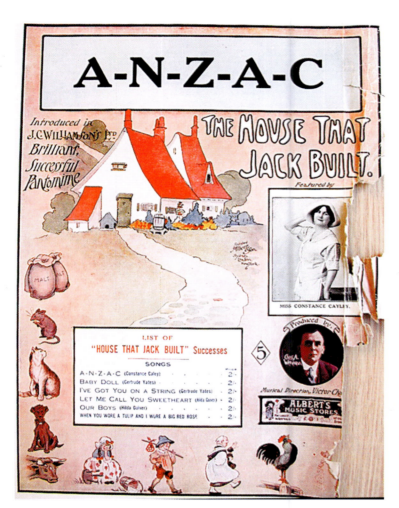

In April 1917, Allan & Co., Melbourne, wanted to bring out sheet music called 'Songs of Anzac'. To support their request, they attached to their letter to the Attorney General this sheet music featuring a series of songs entitled 'A-N-Z-A-C'. Permission was granted.
(NAA. A432/86, 29/3484 Pt.14).

In 1916, Kops Brewery, Brisbane, manufactured the 'Anzac Toast', a non-alcoholic drink. Kops had produced a large quantity of 'Anzac Toast' labels and asked to be allowed to use them until the end of the run. They were refused.
(NAA. A432/86, 29/3484 Pt.17).

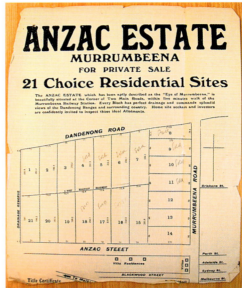

In September 1916, the Commonwealth instructed Mr E G Batchelor, Bendigo, that the word Anzac 'must be obliterated from the posters' he was using to advertise land sales at the Anzac Estate. (NAA. A432/86, 1929/3484 Pt.19).

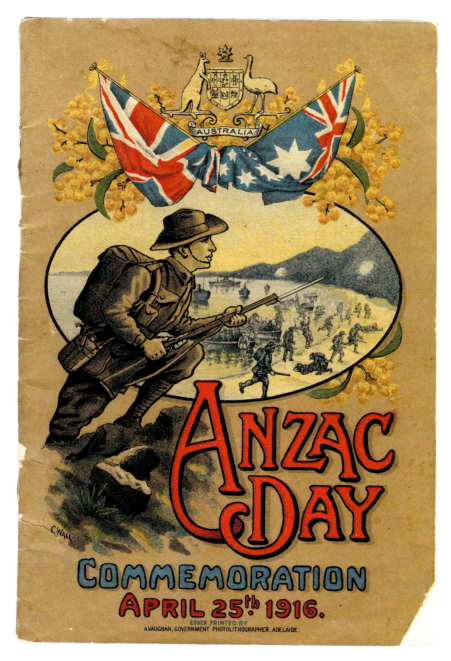

LEFT: Front cover of an Anzac Day souvenir program, South Australian State War Council, April 1916. Published after Anzac Day, Tuesday, 25 April 1916, the program contents recorded and described the 'Celebrations' which had been held in Adelaide to mark Anzac Day. (AWM).

The soldier image from Harold Cavill's New Year card 'Dinkum Anzac' appeared on the front cover of his book *Imperishable Anzacs: a story of Australia's 1st Brigade*. The book, dedicated to 'Mothers, wives and sisters', was based on Cavill's diary of his time with the 2nd Battalion, AIF, on Gallipoli. (NAA. A1861/1, item 3740).

RIGHT: After 1915, much material was produced at local level about Gallipoli. Peter Wallace, Sale, Victoria, a Boer War veteran, published this patriotic story about a Gippsland father and son who died fighting together at Anzac. (Sale Museum, Victoria).

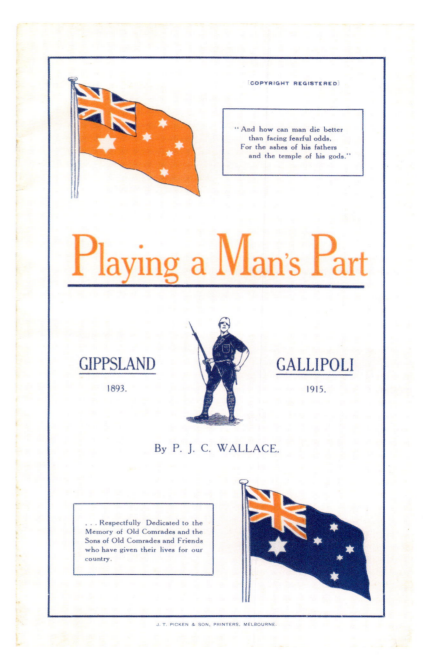

REMEMBERING GALLIPOLI

143

Philip Schuler's *The Battlefields of Anzac*, Melbourne, March 1916. This album featured the photographs of Melbourne journalist Philip Schuler, who had reported from Gallipoli for *The Age*. He subsequently joined the AIF and was killed in France in 1917. (SLNSW).

Bivouac of 4th Inf. Brig. at foot of Sari Bair ridge. Brig.-Gen. Monash, with Lt.-Col. M'Glynn, preparing to occupy a German Officer's dugout and camp.

In the long communication sap that ran from Anzac to the No. 2 Outpost, and afterwards to the New Zealand headquarters. It was 8ft. deep; two donkeys could just pass in it.

Down by the famous Well at No. 2 Post, captured from the Turks, afterwards responsible for supplying 20,000 Troops and 4,000 mules with water daily. A dangerous spot on account of sniping. Captain Bean talking with Col. Bauchop.

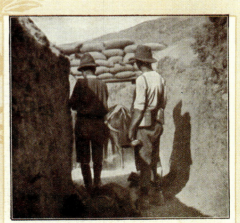

Showing overhead cover of sandbags in the great sap to prevent Turkish sniping. Along this hot, dusty sap all the wounded had to be carried, unless they could walk, after the fighting, 7th to 11th August.

Page opening from Philip Schuler's *The Battlefields of Anzac*. In the top right hand photograph is Charles Bean standing in what was known as the 'Long Sap'. This deep trench ran all the way from just north of Ari Burnu point inland from North Beach to the so-called Outposts, the most northerly part of the Anzac position before the advances made during the 'August Offensive'. The 'Long Sap' was deep enough to protect men from Turkish sniper fire. (SLNSW).

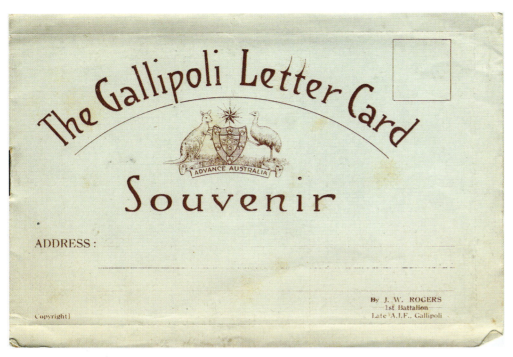

*The Gallipoli Letter Card*, a souvenir history of Gallipoli produced by J W Rogers, ex-1st Battalion, AIF. This is probably Private Joseph William Rogers who joined the 1st Battalion, AIF, in May 1915 and could have served at Gallipoli as a reinforcement for that unit. He returned to Australia in April 1916. (SLNSW).

*Ari Burnu Cemetery, named from the Cape at the North end of Anzac Cove, was made in 1915 ... It covers an area of 2,181 square yards; and it contains the graves of 148 soldiers from Australia (82 of whom belonged to the Light Horse), 33 from New Zealand, 27 (including sailors of the Royal Naval Division and from the Fleet) from the United Kingdom, and 37 whose unit in our forces is not known. One man from the Maltese Labour Corps is buried in Row J. The names of three soldiers from Australia and two from New Zealand, for whom there is evidence of burial in this cemetery, are recorded on special tablets; and the other tablets record the names of three Indian soldiers who were buried in Kilid Bahr. The cemetery lies between the beach and the cliff, under Plugge's Plateau. It is surrounded on three sides by a belt of pines and on the fourth, where it faces the sea, by an ashlar rubble wall.*

[Commonwealth War Graves Commission, Cemetery Register, Ari Burnu Cemetry, Gallipoli]

TOP: Lieutenant Cyril Hughes (left), AIF and British Graves Registration Unit, Gallipoli, and Sergeant Arthur Woolley, AIF, marking out graves in Brown's Dip cemetery, Anzac, March 1919. Later in 1919, the Imperial War Graves Commission put Hughes, a Gallipoli veteran, in charge of all post-war cemetery and memorial construction on Gallipoli. (AWM G01935).

LEFT: No. 1 and No. 2 cemeteries at Brown's Dip, Anzac, 1919, with crosses erected by the British Graves Registration Unit. These graves were later removed to the Lone Pine Cemetery. (AWM G01849).

TOP LEFT: Burial party in 1918 cremating the remains of Ghurka soldiers killed on Gallipoli in 1915. (AWM H02917).

TOP RIGHT: Soldiers' bones and equipment litter the ground in March 1919 at the head of the Aghyl Dere where the British Army's 38th Infantry Brigade, under General A H Baldwin, suffered huge losses on the morning of 10 August 1915. (AWM G02002).

LEFT: Turkish bones and skulls, Gallipoli 1919. (AWM H11907).

*Here at once we came on groups of our dead, some with the colours of the 14th battalion on their sleeves. One group lay as far up the ridge as Hill 100 — Australians and Turks together; one had the badge or colour of the 14th Battalion, and one a small Bible with the name 'H Wellington' on the fly leaf.*

[Charles Bean, official Australian war historian]

*Thus as we rode northwards along this road the trenches were never, except where a gully broke them, more than fifty yards away on either hand … It gave a strange thrill to ride along this space in front of Steel's, Courtney's and Quinn's where three years before men could not even crawl at night. The bones and tattered uniforms of men were scattered everywhere.*

[Charles Bean, official Australian war historian]

Members of the Australian Historical Mission, 1919, led by Charles Bean (second from left), contemplating the short distance between the opposing trenches at Lone Pine. Behind the group on the skyline is the Turkish monument to the Battle of Lone Pine. (AWM G01946).

TOP RIGHT: Turkish monument erected on Lone Pine after the Allied evacuation, in memory of their men who died while attempting to recapture the position taken by the 1st Infantry Brigade, AIF, on 6 August 1915. (AWM G01752).

*I saw now, with something of a shock … a monument put up by the Turks to mark the spot* [at Lone Pine] *at which they had stopped the terrific August thrust. Away on the ridges nearly a mile beyond it, at The Nek where also we had been stopped, we could see another monument (and we afterwards noted a third at North Beach). Obviously the Turks were very proud of their achievement. And, we reflected, those who stopped the invading spearheads on Gallipoli well deserved commemoration as soldiers and patriots.*

[Charles Bean, official Australian war historian]

After the war families could ask for details of the grave of a loved one. These were supplied in the form of a card specifying the cemetery and a photograph of the temporary cross on the grave. Private William O'Brien, 6th Light Horse Regiment, was killed in action on Gallipoli on 12 July 1917. (AWM P0741.03.02).

BELOW: The Special Memorial in Lone Pine Cemetery for Private Ronald Ernest Coates, 2nd Battalion, AIF, killed during the Battle of Lone Pine. A Special Memorial indicates that Coates' actual grave is unknown but that he is most likely buried at Lone Pine. (AWM H16822).

*Gladly Did I Live And Gladly Die And I Laid Me Down With A Will*

[Inscription, Ari Burnu Cemetery, grave of Lieutenant Edward Henty, 8th Light Horse Regiment, AIF, killed in action at the Nek, 7 August 1915]

*After perhaps all great wars — certainly after all modern ones — soldiers and relatives and, later, interested visitors have flowed to the battlefields; and one's mind could see Anzac, the most striking battlefield of that war, being the goal of pilgrimages from Britain and the Anzac countries, a calling place on Mediterranean tours, a regular stopping place for those who visited Egypt and the Holy Land and thence made their way by Damascus and the Taurus to Asia Minor, Constantinople and Greece. Here was a battlefield in which, though the trenches could not be preserved — as was being done in France — the graves themselves would mark the front line and even the farthest lines reached in the struggle so heroic on both sides.*

[Charles Bean, official Australian war historian]

An early, unidentified pilgrim to Gallipoli - the wife of a soldier placing a wreath at Ari Burnu Cemetery, Anzac Cove, 25 April 1923. (AWM H12950).

*Well! We're gone. We're out of it all! We've somewhere else to fight.*
*And we strain our eyes from the transport deck, but 'Anzac' is out of sight!*
*Valley and shore have vanished; vanished are cliff and hill;*
*And we'll never go back to 'Anzac' … But I think that some of us will!*

[From 'Anzac', Major Oliver Hogue, 6th Light Horse Regiment, AIF]

First reunion, Hobart, 18 October 1930, of the first Tasmanian contingent, AIF. These men sailed from Hobart on 20 October 1914 in the transports *Geelong* and *Katuna* and it is likely that virtually all of them became Anzacs. (AWM P210.02).

# ACKNOWLEDGMENTS

I would like to acknowledge the assistance of the following people in the writing and production of this book: from the Department of Veterans' Affairs, Courtney Page-Allen for picture research and caption drafts, Kerry Blackburn and Bob Pounds for advice and encouragement at all times and Ian Skinner for photographic support; staff of the Australian War Memorial, especially Ian Affleck, Andrew Jack, Jillian Brankin and Brad Manera; the team at ABC Books, especially Jenny Mills and Melanie Feddersen of i2i Design who gave much more than was asked to this project.

Thanks also to the following institutions for providing photographs from their collections: Australian War Memorial; National Archives of Australia; National Library of Australia; Sale Museum; State Library of New South Wales. Please note that the following abbreviations have been used in crediting the images.

AWM:            Australian War Memorial
NAA:            National Archives Australia
NLA:            National Library of Australia
SLNSW:          State Library of New South Wales

COVER IMAGES: front cover. AWM; back cover AWM; back flap NLA.
ENDPAPERS: AWM

The poem on page ii is believed to be by Captain James Spent, 3rd Field Ambulance, AIF.

# BIBLIOGRAPHY

Alexander, Major H. M. *On Two Fronts: Being the Adventures of an Indian Mule Corps in France and Gallipoli.* William Heineman, London, n.d.

Allanson, Lieutenant Colonel Cyril. 1/6th Gurkha Rifles, *Campaigning in Gallipoli*, AWM copy, n.d.

*Ashmead-Bartlett's Despatches from the Dardanelles.* George Newnes, London, 1916.

Barwick, Private A. 1st Battalion, AIF. Diary, Mss 1493, Mitchell Library, State Library of New South Wales.

Bean, Charles.
   'Official dispatches from Gallipoli',
   *Commonwealth of Australia Gazette,* 1915.
   *Gallipoli Mission.* ABC Books, Sydney, 1990.
   *The Story of Anzac.* vol.I, Angus and Robertson, Sydney, 1935.
   *The Story of Anzac.* vol.II, Angus and Robertson, 1924.

Beeston, Joseph. *Five Months at Anzac.* Angus and Robertson, Sydney, n.d.

Belford, W. C. *Legs Eleven, being the story of the 11th Battalion (AIF) in the Great War of 1914-1918.* Imperial Printing Company, Perth, 1940.

Blenkinsop, Major General Sir L J and Lieutenant Colonel J. W. Rainey (eds), *History of the Great War Based on Official Documents: Veterinary Services.* His Majesty's Stationery Office, London, 1925.

Butler, A. G. *Official History of the Australian Army Medical Services, 1914-1918, Gallipoli, Palestine and New Guinea.* vol.1, Australian War Memorial, Canberra, 1930.

Collett, Colonel Herbert. *The 28th, a Record of the War Service with the Australian Imperial Force, 1915-1919.* Trustees Public Library, Perth, 1922.

Cowen, James. *The Maoris in the Great War: A History of The New Zealand Native Contingent and Pioneer Battalion,* Whitcombe and Tombs, Auckland, 1926.

Denning, Roy. *My Dear Mother: A letter from a soldier after Gallipoli.* Yass and District Historical Society, Yass, NSW, 1999.

Donnell, Anne. *Letters of an Army Sister.* Angus and Robertson, Sydney, 1920.

East, Sir R (ed). *The Gallipoli Diary of Sergeant Lawrence of the Australian Engineers, 1st AIF, 1915.* Melbourne University Press, Melbourne, 1981.

Gammage, Bill. *The Broken Years: Australian Soldiers in the Great War.* Penguin, Sydney, 1975.

Herbert, Aubrey. *Mons, Anzac and Kut.* Edward Arnold, London, 1919.

Hogue, Oliver. *Trooper Bluegum at the Dardanelles.* Andrew Melrose, London, 1915.

Jackson, Sergeant H. M. 13th Battalion, AIF. Diary, 1DRL/0379, Australian War Memorial, Canberra.

James, Robert Rhodes. *Gallipoli.* Pimlico, London, 1999.

Laird, J. T. *Other Banners: An anthology of Australian literature of the First World War.* Australian War Memorial, Canberra, 1971.

Liddle, Peter. *Men of Gallipoli.* David and Charles, Newton Abbot, 1988.

Longmore, Captain Cyril. *The Old Sixteenth, Being a Record of the 16th Battalion, AIF, During the Great War, 1914-1918.* History Committee 16th Battalion, Perth, 1929.

Moorehead, Alan. *Gallipoli.* Woodsworth Editions, Ware, 1997.

Murray, Joseph. *Gallipoli 1915.* Nell Paperbacks, London, 1977.

Pugsley, Chris. *Gallipoli: The New Zealand Story.* Reed Publishing, Sydney, 1998.

Rusden, Corporal William, New Zealand Expeditionary Force. Letter, 3DRL/2287, Australian War Memorial, Canberra.

Silas, Ellis. 'The Diary of an Anzac'. Unpublished manuscript, Mitchell Library Mss.1840, State Library of New South Wales.

Tyquin, M. *Gallipoli: The Medical War.* NSW University Press, Sydney, 1993.

Wilson H. W. and J A Hammerton (eds), *The Great War: The Standard History of the All-Europe Conflict.* The Amalgamated Press, London, 1915.

Waite, Major Fred. *The New Zealanders at Gallipoli.* Whitcombe and Tombs , Auckland, 1921.

The view from Walker's Ridge at sundown on a fine day was hard to beat: its peaceful beauty ought never to have been disturbed by the din of battle. Anzac would have been a splendid holiday resort in happier times, with its grand climate in the early summer months: fine golf links could be laid out along the stretch between the old position and Suvla. There is good sea-fishing, too; and those rugged hills must surely contain some kinds of game, while the sea bathing is of the very best — the water clear and warm, and deep within a few yards of the shore.

[Major H M Alexander, Indian Mule Transport Corps]